Anonymus

Commissioners of Public Works (Ireland)

Sixty-third report with appendices

Anonymus

Commissioners of Public Works (Ireland)
Sixty-third report with appendices

ISBN/EAN: 9783742810465

Manufactured in Europe, USA, Canada, Australia, Japa

Cover: Foto ©Suzi / pixelio.de

Manufactured and distributed by brebook publishing software
(www.brebook.com)

Anonymus

Commissioners of Public Works (Ireland)

PUBLIC WORKS, IRELAND.

SIXTY-THIRD ANNUAL REPORT

OF THE

COMMISSIONERS OF PUBLIC WORKS

IN

IRELAND:

WITH

APPENDICES,

FOR THE YEAR ENDING 31ST MARCH, 1895.

Presented to both Houses of Parliament by Command of Her Majesty.

DUBLIN:
PRINTED FOR HER MAJESTY'S STATIONERY OFFICE,
BY ALEXANDER THOM & CO. (LIMITED).

And to be purchased, either directly or through any Bookseller, from
HODGES, FIGGIS, and Co. (Limited), 104, Grafton-street, Dublin; or
EYRE and SPOTTISWOODE, East Harding-street, Fleet-street, E.C.; or
JOHN MENZIES and Co., 12, Hanover-street, Edinburgh, and 90, West Nile-street, Glasgow.

1895.

[C.—7819.] *Price 8d*

TABLE OF CONTENTS.

REPORT AND APPENDICES.

APPENDICES—*continued.*

PUBLIC WORKS, IRELAND.

SIXTY-THIRD ANNUAL REPORT

OF THE

COMMISSIONERS OF PUBLIC WORKS IN IRELAND,

FOR THE YEAR 1894-95.

TO THE LORDS COMMISSIONERS OF HER MAJESTY'S TREASURY.

MAY IT PLEASE YOUR LORDSHIPS,

IN submitting our Sixty-third Annual Report we propose to adhere to the arrangement of subjects adopted in the Report of last year.

(1.) Voted Services, *i.e.*, services for which provision is made by vote of Parliament.

(2.) Light Railways and Tramways.

(3.) Non-voted Services, *i.e.*, services provided for from other sources than Parliamentary votes.

(4.) Loans.

A general statement of the duties of the Board will be found on page 24 of this Report.

We proceed to submit some general observations with reference to each of the four divisions above set forth.

I.—VOTED SERVICES.

Under this head of our duties, comprising the services which are created by, or maintained from, annual votes of Parliament, the accounts record the following net expenditures on each to 31st March, 1895, and the second column shows the net expenditure on the same votes for the preceding year 1893-94:— I.—Voted Services.

—	1894-95.	1893-94.
Class I. Public Works and Buildings, and Railways, Ireland. .	£ 376,357	£ 469,383
Class II. Public Works Office, ...	36,388	36,298
	412,745	505,681

These services comprise —

Public Buildings, Ireland, viz. :—

Naval and Military; State and Official Residences; Civil Departments; Legal Departments; Metropolitan Police; Royal Irish Constabulary; Dundrum Criminal Lunatic Asylum; Science and Art Department; Public Education; Royal University and Queen's Colleges; Revenue Departments.

Royal Parks and Gardens :—

Phœnix Park; St. Stephen's green; The Curragh of Kildare.

Royal Harbours :—

Kingstown; Howth; Donaghadee; Dunmore; Ardglass.

Inland Navigations :—

Boyne; Maigue.

Ancient Monuments Protection Act, 1882, 45 & 46 Vic., c. 73.

Ditto, Ditto, 1892, 55 & 56 Vic., c. 46.

Tramways and Light Railways—See also II., page 8.

PUBLIC BUILDINGS.

The Public Buildings in charge of the Board are made up as follows:—

Naval and Military Buildings,	371
Revenue Departments,	146
State and Official Residences,	17
Other Civil Departments,	1,007

Dundrum Central Criminal Lunatic Asylum.—This Asylum was erected many years ago upon a plan which it has since been found necessary to adapt to modern requirements. A scheme of improvement for that purpose has been undertaken after consultation with the Inspectors of Lunatic Asylums, and has for some time been in continuous progress with such modifications, both as to the details of the work and the order of its execution as were from time to time suggested by the department referred to. The expenditure is being spread over several years. Parts of the boundary wall have been rebuilt or raised in order to diminish the risk of escape by inmates. It has, however, been considered desirable to postpone for the present further action in this direction in order to proceed with works calculated to improve the sanitary condition of the establishment, and to facilitate administration and the enforcement of discipline.* In furtherance of the programme of improvement new sewage disposal works have been carried out, and one of the places of worship belonging to the Institution has been removed to a position external to the main building in order to allow of the space thus set free being utilized for other purposes. During the year 1894–5 the Board completed the re-arrangement of the quarters occupied by female inmates. This consisted in substituting cells for the previous open dormitory accommodation, building a sanitary annexe, and carrying out certain minor works.

Extensive new stores have also been built within the year. On their completion according to the designs adopted, after consultation with the Inspectors of Lunatic Asylums, several valuable improvements involving considerable extra cost were suggested by them to the Board, and the necessary expenditure having been sanctioned by your Lordships, they were fully carried out before the close of the year. Provision has been made for further progress in the present year, during which it is proposed that extensive improvements shall be made on the male side. The heating of the Asylum and other works, with the question of the boundary wall, will remain to be dealt with hereafter, subject to your Lordships' sanction, in such order as may be determined on.

New Parcel Post Depot, Amiens-street.—The Dublin Parcel Post Depot has now been completed with the exception of the permanent electric lighting plant which is under contract. The site adjoins the junction of the Great Northern and Dublin Junction Railway Companies at Amiens-street Terminus, and is in direct communication with all parts of the United Kingdom.

The building, which was designed by the Board's Senior Surveyor, will be completed for the original estimate of £16,500. It is built of red brick and cut stone, and consists on the street and basement levels of a van yard approached from Preston-street, 70 feet by 50 feet, to which adjoin extensive stores, sorters' rooms, sanitary accommodation, and an engine and boiler house approached from Amiens-street by a separate entrance and yard. On the ground floor are a public office, 45 feet by 28 feet, approached from Amiens-street, a local sorting office, 70 feet square, adjoining the van-yard platform, approached from Preston-street, and registered parcels and private offices. The first floor consists of offices for the directing staff, and the principal sorting office, which is 120 feet by 70 feet.

A staircase and two hydraulic lifts connect the several floors, and the principal sorting office is connected with the platforms of the Great Northern and Dublin Junction Railway Companies, on each of which is a hydraulic lift, by a steel lattice girder bridge, through which trucks convey the parcels from the lifts in the Depot to those on the platforms. The boilers, which evaporate about 1,800 lbs. of steam per hour at a pressure of 100 lbs. on the square inch, supply two Tangye pumps working against a hydraulic pressure of 700 lbs. on the square inch into an accumulator which works the four lifts. The boilers are also intended to supply two steam dynamos. These supply a direct current of 100 volts to a central switch board in the principal sorting office, from which the whole of the electric lighting circuits can be economically controlled. The current is distributed on a Concentric System, which has been here used for the first time in Ireland. The building was completed in November, and the full advantage of the accommodation, fittings, and machinery utilised for the transaction of business at Christmas.

* Since the above was written arrangements have been made for proceeding with the raising of the boundary walls.

Electric Lighting.—The Board have two large installations with independent plant, one at the Science and Art Buildings in Kildare-street, complete for some years, and the other already referred to at the Parcel Post Depôt approaching completion. The former was erected under the advice of Mr. Preece, Engineer to the G.P.O. London. The Science and Art installation works satisfactorily from the point of view of efficiency and economy, and there is every reason to anticipate similar results from that in course of completion at the Parcels Depôt. The supervision of the plant and the design and specification of all the recent works have been carried out in the department.

Before deciding on the erection of an independent plant at the Parcel Post Depôt, the Board negociated for the supply with the Electric Lighting Committee of the Dublin Corporation. After the terms of supply had been discussed and an understanding arrived at on the principal items, the Corporation satisfied the Board that the supply would have to be postponed to a time considerably later than that originally contemplated, and as the delay would have been a source of expense and inconvenience it was determined to erect independent plant.

The Lighting of the Accountant's Branch of the General Post Office has also been the subject of communications with the Committee of the Corporation. The wiring of the building has been completed for some time past and everything is ready for the current. The Committee have a difficulty in supplying it at present. If necessary, independent plant can be introduced, as in the Parcel Post Depôt. The State Apartments at Dublin Castle were wired some few years since, and have been worked during the season by plant specially hired every year. It is hoped that the necessary supply will be soon obtainable from the Electric Lighting Committee.

Speaking generally it is found that independent installations are a source of economy except where the number of lamps is small or the hours of lighting short.

Grants in aid of Erection and Improvement of National Schools.—The vote for grants to aid in the erection and improvement of National Schools was £28,000. The entire of this sum with an excess of about £150 was expended. Reference was made in our last two Reports to the difficulties arising from uncertainty as to the time at which grants sanctioned by the Commissioners of National Education became payable actually to the managers of schools. The cause of this is the course sometimes adopted by managers of postponing works for an indefinite time after sanction of a grant has been intimated. This leads in one year to the non-expenditure of part of the sum voted by Parliament and in another to an expenditure in excess of that sum. We are happy to state that as the result of conference with the Department of National Education during the latter part of the year measures are under arrangement to remedy the inconveniences referred to, which pressed on managers as much as on the Departments concerned. It is proposed that conditions involving no hardship, but calculated to strengthen the hands of managers in carrying out buildings and improvements, shall henceforth be attached to the grants. Suggestions with reference to contracts and matters of detail will also be made to them, and no doubt acted on. With their co-operation we have every reason to hope that the service will be placed on a satisfactory footing.

PHŒNIX PARK.

In the Report of last year we referred to the extent to which the Park roads had been used for business as distinguished from pleasure traffic. We noticed particularly their use by market gardeners' carts, farmers' carts, and traders' vans. The question of the construction of a road by the Grand Jury of the County Dublin which would relieve the Park from what may be called agricultural traffic was brought before the last Presentment sessions by cesspayers resident in the locality interested, but was withdrawn from immediate consideration in consequence of some defects in procedure. It is understood that the subject will be renewed, and in the meantime the market gardeners frequenting the Dublin markets are furnished with temporary passes enabling them to drive through the Park.

With regard to vans, &c., delivering goods from city establishments the experience given by the restrictive measures adopted in the beginning of 1894, in order to place some check on the excessive and unnecessary use previously made of the Park roads for such purposes has enabled the Board to measure fully the real necessities of the case. A system of passes has now been adopted which is found to satisfy the requirements of traders and their customers without involving the excessive use of the roads for business traffic which formerly prevailed.

The public cricket ground, the preparation of which was commenced in 1893, is getting into good condition, and there is every reason to hope that it will be largely used and give satisfaction.

In connection with this the Board desire to refer to the absence of legal power on their part (such as exists in England under the Parks Regulations Acts) to ensure the protection of such improvements as the public cricket ground, and to preserve them as also other portions of the Park from injury, whether resulting from carelessness or from malice. The want has long been recognised but it will be felt more acutely according as spaces are specially prepared by the Board for the use of the public for various pastimes, *e.g.*, for a children's gymnasium which they would otherwise gladly have carried out. They venture to suggest that there is need of a statutory power to make bye-laws for the purpose indicated subject to such restrictions and conditions as to confirmation as may be thought desirable. Power already exists for making and enforcing bye-laws deemed necessary by the police for the regulation of traffic. While making the above suggestion the Board desire to bear testimony to the spirit in which the public generally frequenting the parks and gardens under their management have co-operated to keep those places in good order.

KINGSTOWN HARBOUR.

During the year a contract was entered into for the construction of an entirely new roofing for the Mail Packet Pier, covering a considerably larger space than the old roof. Good progress has been made with the work, which it is hoped will be completed shortly. The extended protection which it will afford to passengers and mails was urgently needed.

The pump dredger contracted for in the previous financial year was delivered in September last, since which time it has done good service, having raised and removed at very moderate cost some 57,000 tons of spoil from the harbour.

A contract was also placed for a smaller dredger, with grab, which was delivered at Kingstown in March. By the aid of this machine it is hoped to reduce considerably the cost of removing material for which the pump dredger is not adapted.

BOYNE NAVIGATION.

The Boyne Navigation was one of the systems of Inland Navigation constructed with the aid of grants from the Irish Parliament. On the failure of the undertakers to complete the system from Drogheda to Trim, the lower section, from Drogheda to Carrickdexter Lock, passed into the control of the State; and the upper section, from that Lock to Navan, into the hands of the River Boyne Company. This division of control and the competition of railways was not favourable to the maintenance, still less the development of the traffic. While the lower section was properly maintained by this Board, out of funds annually provided by Parliament, the upper, owing to the insufficiency of the revenue to cover expenditure, gradually fell into disrepair. As the whole traffic was thus threatened with extinction the Board took steps to interest the merchants of Navan and Drogheda in the maintenance of the Navigation. A new Company, to take over both sections, has been formed, to which the Drogheda S.S. Company contributes £1,200, and the Treasury a free grant of £3,500. A Bill to confirm this arrangement was introduced in the last Session, and will be proceeded with in the new Parliament, and we have every hope that the Navigation to Navan will be maintained and become of increasing benefit to the locality.

II.—LIGHT RAILWAYS AND TRAMWAYS.

TRAMWAYS AND LIGHT RAILWAYS UNDER THE ACTS OF 1860 to 1890.

Light Railways and Tramways.

Our Report of last year contained a full statement of the operation of these Acts and of the history of railway progress in Ireland so far as it is affected by State or local aid. The work for which assistance was provided under the Tramways Act of 1883 and the Light Railways Act of 1889 is nearly completed. Before mentioning the portions of it carried out during the year 1894-5, we desire to state succinctly the main object of each of the Acts passed on this complex subject from 1860, so far as they affect this Board.

1. The Tramways Act of 1860 (23 & 24 Vic., c. 152).—This Act dealt mainly with procedure. It made no provision to enable either the local authorities or the Treasury to aid financially the construction of railways. It imposed on us the duty of inquiring into "the merits of the undertaking."

II. The Tramways Act of 1861 (24 & 25 Vic., c. 102).—This Act was also confined to matter of procedure, and had no financial provisions bearing on the local authority or the Treasury.

It restricted (ss. 6 & 7) the inquiry by the Board into the merits of the undertakings to engineering questions.

III. The Relief of Distress Amendment Act, 1880 (43 & 44 Vic., c. 14), empowered the Treasury to lend on special terms, on the security of a baronial guarantee, for the construction of lines specified in a schedule to the Act.

IV. The Tramways and Public Companies (Ireland) Act, 1883, enabled Grand Juries to charge baronies or parts of baronies in perpetuity, or for a period, with interest not exceeding 5 per cent., on the capital required for the construction of Tramways or Light Railways (Sec. 1). The effect of the presentment affecting this charge (when confirmed by Order of the Lord Lieutenant in Council) was twofold—(1) it bound the districts charged to make good the ascertained half yearly deficiency in the net receipts to the amount of such interest; (2) it also rendered the districts chargeable, under certain circumstances specified in the Act, with the payment from time to time of such sums as might be required for completing, working, or maintaining the undertaking.

It further enabled the Treasury to repay the district half the amount duly paid by it under the guarantee given by Sec. 9, provided—(1) that the line was maintained in order and used for traffic; (2) that the Treasury payment should not exceed 2 per cent. on the capital guaranteed.

The liability of the Treasury was limited to an annuity of £40,000 per annum.

V. The Light Railways Act, 1889, enabled the State to aid the construction of Light Railways by—(a) a capital sum, which might be a grant or loan, or partly one and partly the other; (b) an annual payment; (c) capital sum and annual payment combined.

It rendered this aid available for such railways as the Lord Lieutenant in Council might from time to time declare to be desirable between certain places for the development of fisheries and other industries, and to require (owing to the circumstances of the district) special assistance from the State for their construction.

The State assistance was to be derived—(a) from the unappropriated balance of the annuity of £40,000 given by the Tramways and Public Companies Act, 1883; (b) from a capital sum of £600,000 to be provided by Parliament; (c) from an additional annuity of £2,000. The adjustment of the two forms of aid, annual payment and capital sum, so as not to exceed the limits of the Treasury assistance already stated, was directed to be made on the basis of 3 per cent.

The Act was to apply only—(a) where the promoters of the Light Railways are an Irish Railway Company having a railway open for traffic; or (b) where the promoters have made an agreement approved by the Treasury for the maintenance, management, and working of the Light Railway by such Railway Company; or (c) where a baronial guarantee was given for the payment of dividends upon a portion of the capital pursuant to the provisions of the Act of 1883.

VI. The Railways (Ireland) Act, 1890, was passed for the purpose of enabling special sessions to be held to consider certain Railway schemes mentioned in the First Schedule to the Act.

Section 5 of this Act authorized the construction of a railway other than a light railway under any agreement made by the Treasury with a Railway Company under Sec. 4 of the Act of 1889.

VII. The Transfer of Railways (Ireland) Act, 1890, gave powers for the transfer to and vesting in a Railway Company of any undertaking that had obtained a presentment under the Tramways (Ireland) Acts.

It provided that baronial guarantees were to remain in force, and the Railway Company to which the transfer might be made was authorized to issue baronial guaranteed shares, and themselves to guarantee punctual payment of dividends; or in lieu of such shares, to create and issue debenture stock equal in amount to the guaranteed stock, the Company being regarded as the holder of the guaranteed stock unissued and entitled to receive the dividends thereon.

Section 17 of the same Act gave power to the promoters of any light railway with whom the Treasury had made an agreement to enter upon any land which they were authorized to take on depositing in the Bank of Ireland such sum as may be certified to be proper by a valuer appointed by the Board of Public Works.

VIII. The Public Accounts and Charges Act, 1891, enabled the permanent annuities created under the Act of 1883 to be capitalised, and the equivalent sum borrowed from the National Debt Commissioners to be repaid by temporary annuities.

IX. The Light Railways (Ireland) Act, 1893, sanctioned an increase of the annuities authorized by the previous Acts by further annuities to the amount of £5,000.

As shown in the annexed table, of the lines to which State assistance was given under the Acts of 1889 and 1893, only the Collooney and Claremorris line remains uncompleted. The difficulties as regards the junctions at the terminal stations, which have been the cause of so much delay, have now been removed, and we anticipate the opening of the line for traffic at an early date.

LIGHT RAILWAYS ACTS, 1889 AND 1893.

No.	Name of Road.	Length.	Remarks.
		Miles.	
1	Donegal and Killybegs, . .	18½	Opened for traffic in 1893.
2	Stranorlar and Glenties, . .	24½	Opened for traffic, 1895.
3	Ballina and Killala, . .	8	Opened for traffic in 1893.
4	Westport and Mallaranny, .	18	Opened for traffic, 1894.
5	Achill Extension, ...	8¼	Opened for traffic, 1895.
6	Collooney and Claremorris, . .	47	Almost completed.
7	Galway and Clifden, . . .	48¼	Opened for traffic, 1895.
8	Killorglin and Valentia, . . .	26¾	Opened for traffic, 1893.
9	Headford and Kenmare, . .	19¾	Opened for traffic, 1893.
10	Baltimore and Skibbereen, . .	7¾	Opened for traffic, 1893.
11	Bantry Extension, ...	1¼	Opened for traffic, 1892.
12	Downpatrick and Ardglass, . .	8	Opened for traffic in 1892.

III.—NON-VOTED SERVICES.

This head includes the following items:—

Arterial Drainage Works.
Arterial Drainage, Maintenance and Increased Rents.
Railway Gauges Consolidation Act.
Fishery Piers and Harbours Acts, 1846 to 1893.
Fishery Piers and Harbours Maintenance.
Arklow Harbour.
Shannon Navigation.
Sea and Coast Fisheries (Ireland) Loan Fund.
National Monuments and Ecclesiastical Ruins.
Post Road Repairs.
County Surveyors' Assistants.
Bridges between Counties.
Limited Owners' Residences.
Arbitrations—For Railways and other Public Works.
Loans—Receivers' Accounts.

This division of our duties comprises a variety of services placed under our control or management in pursuance of several Acts of Parliament. Though numerous, most of them are of only casual occurrence, and therefore do not form the subject of any special remarks, with the exception of the case of the Suck Drainage.

River Suck Drainage.

A scheme prepared by Mr. Lynam, C.E., for the drainage of the River Suck was promoted under the Drainage and Improvement of Lands Act (Ireland), 1863, in the year 1875. The estimate of total cost was £120,287, equal to an annuity of £6,118 for 35 years; of lands improved 21,040 acres, of improved value of £7,852. The scheme however failed to obtain the necessary proportion of assents, and in March, 1877, a reduced scheme was promoted by, among others, the O'Conor Don, Messrs. Wills Sandford, E. W. Fowler, agent for Lord Clancarty, G. A. Holmes, agent for C. Neville Bagot, St. George Caulfield, &c. The scheme was examined by Mr. Forsyth as Inspector, and the estimate of lands improved was returned as 19,005 acres, of improved value £5,087, of cost £103,690.

The requisite proportion of assents having been received, the Drainage District was constituted by a Provisional Order dated 27th February, 1878, which was confirmed by the Local Act 41 V., c. 88, Drainage and Improvement of Lands Supplemental Act, (Ireland), 1878.

The period for the completion of the work was limited to the 1st January, 1884; but as time went on it became evident that they could not be finished within the period, although the Board of Works had given an extension of time under their powers. Accordingly, in 1886, an Act was obtained extending the time for the completion of the works, and also containing a novel provision, namely, that in addition to the representatives of the proprietors on the Drainage Board there should also be representatives of the occupiers. This was done by adding seven elected members to the twenty-one members originally on the Board. In course of time it again became evident that even within the extended time provided by the Act of 1886 the works could not be completed; and in 1889 another Act was obtained giving further time for the completion of the works, that is to say, until the 1st January, 1889, with power to the Board of Works to give a further extension, not exceeding three years. There were also several other special provisions—one was that in addition to the sums which under the general Drainage Acts might be charged on the counties in respect of bridges, &c., a further sum of £13,000 should be charged on the County Cess of a limited area to be defined by the Lord Lieutenant by Order in Council. Secondly, Parliament authorized the Treasury to make a free grant of £50,000 towards the cost of the works, and the borrowing powers of the Drainage Board were limited to a sum of £113,000 in addition to the £13,000 and £50,000. Thirdly, the representation of the occupiers was extended to one-half the Drainage Board; that is to say, out of 28 members, 14 were to represent occupiers and 14 landowners. Changes were also made by the Act as to the apportionment of the expense of the works by the Final Award, it being provided that, after deducting the two sums of £13,000 and £50,000 above mentioned, the total cost of the works should be apportioned in two annuities to be called the "occupiers annuity" and the "proprietors annuity," to be paid direct to the Board of Works for a term of 40 years. Under the ordinary Arterial Drainage Acts the proprietors would alone have been responsible to the Board of Works for the repayment of the cost of the work, though they would have been entitled to receive from the tenants such increased rents, not exceeding the estimated value of the improvement effected on each holding, as the Board of Works on their application and after due inquiry might fix. The effect of the Act of 1889, in the case of the River Suck, is to make the occupiers directly responsible to the Board of Works for the payment of an annuity in respect of each holding not exceeding the estimated value of the improvement effected by the Drainage Works. The whole trouble and risk of collection is thus transferred from the proprietors to the Board, and from the number of holdings affected, and the varying amount of the annuities to be collected, it will be seen that a very considerable addition will be made to the work of our Accounts Department. Further legislation became necessary in 1890; and at last, in 1894, the works reached a stage at which it was possible for the Board of Works to frame the draft of the Final Award as required by the Act of 1889. The first point to be settled in connection with the Award was the amount of the occupiers annuity. The Act of 1889 provides that the annuity declared to be chargeable upon the interest of the occupier in any portion of land shall be, but shall not exceed, the estimated increased value thereof resulting from the works. Every possible care was taken to arrive at as true an estimate as possible of the area of land benefited, and the amount of the benefit effected in each case by the Drainage Works. Early in February, 1895, the Draft Award was published, in which the occupiers annuity, that is to say, the actual estimated increase in value, was assessed at £3,199 17s., representing a capital sum of £77,771 9s., and the proprietors annuity at £2,605 9s. 2d., equivalent to a capital sum of £57,899 0s. 10d. These two sums amount to £135,670 9s. 10d., and include interest to 31st October, 1894. In addition there was spent £13,000, charged on the county cess under the Act of 1859, £50,000 free grant, and £1,813 4s. 8d., on county bridges.

The Award affected some 1,900 occupiers and 89 proprietors. In accordance with the Act of 1889 an inquiry into objections to the Award was held by a Member of the Board, commencing at Ballinasloe on March 14th, and terminating at Castlerea on April 6th. About 1,100 cases were heard, and a considerable proportion of the district was subsequently reinspected.

The voluminous evidence and information thus collected has since been under careful consideration, and it is hoped that the Final Award will be completed early in August. By lapse of time a further charge for interest of £1,700 has accrued, which will have to be added to the charge on the proprietors with any sum that may, as the result of the inquiry, be deducted from the charge on the occupiers.

It will thus be seen that the improductive expenditure on this drainage scheme has been very large. This result is attributable in different degrees to the fall in land values since the scheme was promoted; to mistakes in the execution of the works, and to the long time occupied by the Drainage Board in completing them, and it adds another instance to those on which are based the remarks on page 14 of this Report as to the necessity for extreme caution in promoting and care in carrying out any Arterial Drainage Scheme.

Shannon Navigation.—Important legislation which was carried during the year, the subject of this service, is noticed at p. 21.

National Monuments and Ecclesiastical Ruins.

Advantage has been conferred on this branch of the Board's service by an arrangement lately made, under which the Royal Irish Academy and the Royal Society of Antiquarians have deputed experienced members of those bodies to confer with the Board on the works of preservation required in different parts of the country. The former is represented by Mr. Thomas Drew, R.H.A., and by Dr. Edward Perceval Wright; the latter by Lord Walter Fitzgerald and the Rev. Denis Murphy, S.J. Through this arrangement the Board obtain the assistance not only of the gentlemen just referred to, but also through them of members of the learned societies skilled in the history and traditions of each district. Local influence and sympathy are also awakened, which it is hoped will have the effect of saving Monuments from much of the injury resulting from carelessness or mischief. The co-operation enjoyed by the Board affords a substantial guarantee that the work of preservation which is their sole statutory duty shall, without expanding into restoration, be carried out in harmony with the design and character of each Monument.

IV.—LOANS.

(1). Loans secured on Undertakings, *e.g.* :—
- For Inland Navigation, Harbours, Railways, &c., under 1 & 2 Wm. IV., c. 33.
- For Labourers' Dwellings in Towns, and Housing of Working Classes, under Acts of 1866, 1883, 1890, and 1893.

(2). Loans secured on Rates, *e.g.* :—
- To Grand Juries for Roads, Bridges, Piers, Harbours, Lunatic Asylum Buildings, Courthouses, Reformatories, and Industrial Schools.
- For purposes sanctioned by the Public Health Act.
- For Labourers' Dwellings under the Act of 1883.
- For Dispensary Houses.

(3). Loans secured on Lands, *e.g.* :—
- For Arterial Drainage Works.
- For Arterial Drainage Maintenance.
- To Owners for improvement of Lands, viz. :—Drainage, erection of Farm Houses and Buildings, of Dwellings for Agricultural Labourers; Planting for Shelter (10 Vic., c. 32, &c.)
- To Tenants for improvement of their Holdings, viz. :—Drainage, and most of the purposes included in the previous service (44 & 45 Vic., c. 49).
- For Purchase under Land Act, 1870.

(4.) Miscellaneous Loans, e.g.:—

Glebe Loans.
For National School Teachers' Residences.
For Seed Supply under Acts of 1880 and 1890, &c.

(5.) Irish Church Fund Loans—secured on Rates or Lands.

The extent and variety of the purposes for which loans are made by the Board are made clear by the abstract of Accounts of Loans for Public Works given in Appendix (C), with the remarks on the several services following thereon, and as regards the year 1894-5, by the following statement of the different purposes for which loans have been made during the year.

Total Number of Loans for each Class.	Purposes of Loans sanctioned [illegible].	No.	Amount.	Total Amount for each Class.
	Class I.—Loans secured on Undertakings.		£	£
	Harbours,	2	8,500	
11	Labourers' Dwellings,	9	36,275	
				44,700
	Class II.—Loans secured on Rates.			
	Loans to Counties:—			
	County Roads, Bridges, and Piers,	2	1,542	
	Repairs of Fishery Piers,	4	2,008	
	Repairs of Post Roads,	1	1,000	
	Lunatic Asylums Buildings,	16	97,020	
	Loans to Unions:—			
	Public Health Acts,	52	133,906	
	Labourers Acts,	*308	194,183	
393	Dispensary Houses,	13	12,560	
				443,479
	Class III.—Loans secured on Lands.			
	River Drainage, 56 & 57 Vic., c. 62,	1	8,000	
	River Drainage Maintenance,	1	84	
	Land Improvement—Loans to Land Owners,	250	38,344	
	" " Occupiers,	479	40,123	
732	" Preliminary Expenses, 10 Vic., c. 32, s. 15,	1	1,000	
				87,553
	Class IV.—Miscellaneous Loans.			
	Glebe Loans,	36	10,613	
	National School Teachers' Residences,	37	5,836	
	National Schools and Training Colleges,	18	5,419	
93	Sundry,	2	1,844	
				23,713
1,433				£601,634

* Number of Electoral Divisions concerned.

ADVANCES, REPAYMENTS, AND ARREARS.

The earliest mention of Public Works Loans to be found in the Abstract submitted by the Board is in connection with the Statute 57 Geo. III., c. 34, passed in 1817. The total of all loan advances from that date to 31st March, 1895 (with certain loans made under special Acts before 1817), is £40,400,053. Advances, repayments, and arrears.

The classified abstract in Appendix (C), pages 40 and 43, shows how this amount has been disposed of, by repayments, remissions, balances outstanding, &c.

	£
Total Repayments,	26,008,513
Total Remissions,	7,922,225
Written off from Local Loans Fund,	197,414
Outstanding Balances,	6,270,867
	£40,400,053

This outstanding balance is represented in the books of the Office by 26,819 open accounts. The loans are generally in course of repayment by half-yearly instalments.

The advances to borrowers in the year 1894–95 out of moneys advanced by the National Debt Commissioners were £477,718, as against £417,251 in 1893–94, and £460,648 in 1892–93.

The amounts received in the year were £516,491, in repayment of principal, and £246,883 in respect of interest, making together £763,374. Of the latter amount, £722,133 was paid to the National Debt Commissioners, and £41,241 to the Irish Land Commission in discharge of principal and interest of loans made out of the Irish Church Fund.

Issues on the Loan Services generally, during the year, do not call for special remarks. There has, however, been a revival of activity under the Labourers Acts which enable Boards of Guardians to provide dwellings for labourers. This is shown by a comparison of the amount of loans sanctioned during each of the last two years:—

	£
1893/4,	45,190
1894/5,	154,183

Lunatic Asylum Loans.

No. 17 in Abstract, p. 40.

Last year's Report recorded the amended terms given by your Lordships with reference to these loans, under the Public Works Loans Act (No. 3), 1893. Under a previous Act (Public Works Loans Act, 1877) Lunatic Asylum loans bore interest at 3½ per cent., and were repaid by annuity in fourteen years. The Act of 1893 enabled the period to be extended to fifty years, and the interest to be reduced to 3¼ or such other rate as, in the judgment of the Treasury, might be necessary in order to enable the loan to be made without loss to the Exchequer, provided that in determining the period regard should be had to the probable duration and continuing utility of the work in aid of which the loan was required.

The terms fixed by your Lordships under these powers were:—(a) for loans for permanent works and buildings, or for the acquisition of any land, or for any easement connected therewith, &c.—

	Rate of Interest.
If repaid within thirty-five years,	3¼ per cent.
If repaid within fifty years,	3½ "

(b) For loans for furniture, fittings, &c., maximum period of repayment, twenty years: rate of interest, 3¼ per cent.

Before the close of the year under report it was under your Lordships' consideration to make the rate of 3¼ per cent. applicable henceforth to all the loans dealt with by the arrangements made under the Act of 1893, and it is understood that this course is about to be adopted.

It is to be remembered that the rate of interest is liable to be revised, not retrospectively, but with regard to future loans, if at any time the contingency of loss to the Exchequer contemplated by the Act of 1893 becomes, in the judgment of your Lordships, probable.

Having referred to this subject for the purpose of showing the contemplated modification of the arrangements made as to these loans in 1893 with regard to interest, we desire to recall the other important feature in those arrangements by which repayment by annuity has been abandoned, and repayment by equal instalments of principal, with interest on the balance outstanding, substituted for it.

Arterial Drainage.

No. 42 in Abstract, p. 42.

The year was an important one in respect of this service, inasmuch as it witnessed, in the case of the Carrigrohane (Co. Cork) Scheme, the first inquiry into a proposal for the substitution of tenants for landlords under the Drainage and Improvement of Land (Ireland) Act of 1892 (55 & 56 V., c. 65).

The principle and effect of this measure deserve notice, and it is of moment that they should be clearly understood by the occupiers of land. Before the Act of 1892 the power to give or refuse assent to the constitution of an arterial drainage district under the Drainage and Improvement of Land (Ireland) Act, 1863, lay exclusively with the owner or landlord, and with tenants under lease for lives renewable for ever, or under lease having forty years to run, all of whom were termed "Proprietors." The ordinary tenant had no such power. The liability to the Board for advances made for carrying out drainage schemes was similarly regulated. It lay exclusively on the "Proprietors." All that the ordinary tenant could be made liable for was an increase to his rent measured by the improvement found after the execution of the works to have been effected in his holding. The value of this improvement was in each case made the subject of special and close inquiry by the Board, and it sometimes happened that it was less, occasionally considerably less, than the proportion of the cost chargeable to the "Proprietor" in respect of the holding. The tenant was thus safeguarded against excessive charges, and the "Proprietor" alone felt the burden of expenditure exceeding the value of the improvement effected. By the operation of the Act of 1892 these provisions of the Act of 1863 became inoperative in the case of substituted tenants. A tenant who obtains an order substituting him for his landlord as Proprietor obtains the right to record his "assent" to the proposed drainage, and that assent counts for the purpose of forming the majority required for the constitution of the district. In acquiring this right, he entails on himself and his holding a corresponding liability in respect of the cost of the works. This liability is not limited to the value of the improvement effected in his farm, but covers the entire portion of the whole cost of the scheme which, under the Act of 1863, would have been chargeable against his landlord in respect of the holding if substitution had not taken place.

This may be illustrated by supposing a case where the entire cost of the scheme was originally estimated at £10,000 and the improvement to a particular holding at £6 10s. a year (which under an advance repayable in 22 years would have repaid £100 of the £10,000), but where the entire cost ultimately rose to £12,000. Assuming the entire estimated benefit to the holding to have been realised, the tenant would have had his rent increased before the Act of 1892 by £6 10s. a year, while the landlord would have been liable for a rentcharge sufficient to repay £120, amounting (in the case of advances repayable in 22 years) to £7 16s., and would thus have been a loser so far as the holding in question was concerned to the extent of £1 6s. a year. If in future cases the tenant under such circumstances avails himself of the Act of 1892, and in consequence of the refusal of the landlord to assent to the scheme, causes himself to be substituted as Proprietor, he steps into the landlord's responsibilities, and becomes liable not to an increased rent of £6 10s. representing the improvement effected, but to a yearly rent-charge of £7 16s.

The difference between the charge on the substituted tenant and the increase of rent which he would have paid as tenant will be still greater if the improvement effected does not prove to be of the value estimated, which is no uncommon occurrence.

It is to be remembered that the responsibility for obtaining plans and estimates from qualified engineers, for making the contracts in connection with the schemes, and for supervision of the works during execution, rests under Statute entirely with the Local Drainage Boards. The duties of this Board are limited to the following points. They appoint an Inspector to report on the proposal when originally submitted; they consider objections made to it, record the assents and dissents of Proprietors, and if the facts disclose no obstacle to the scheme they, acting on the recommendation of the Inspector, "constitute the district." Their duty, after the Provisional Order has been confirmed, is to advance an instalment of the loan before any work is done, and subsequently when called on by the Drainage Board, at such intervals as the latter find convenient, to cause the works to be visited by their Engineer with a view to determining whether the expenditure made requires the advance of a further instalment of the loan. These visits carry no responsibility for proper execution. They were not intended to constitute a supervision of the work. Such supervision, in order to be of value, must be constant. The Board's Engineer when called to visit the works after an interval of three or six months may find obvious defects or deviations, and refuse to certify for an advance until they are remedied, but the manner in which the work is carried out in detail has been outside his supervision and control. The contractor is liable to the Drainage Board exclusively, and the Engineer of the Board of Works occasionally finds that expense has been increased by financial weakness on the part of the contractor, unexpected difficulties arising from floods, &c., extras, neglect or delay. The result is that the original estimate is exceeded, a further loan is required, and the charge on the district thus increased.

These results are obviously more serious to occupiers of small holdings than to the class which has hitherto generally furnished "Proprietors." The former also run greater risks of the losses referred to. The Proprietors, in the original sense of the word, were a comparatively small body, mainly composed of men of leisure and experience of business on a large scale, from whom the Drainage Boards were chosen. The district where substitution takes place on any large scale will not have these advantages to the same extent. It is hoped, however, that by care in the making of contracts, by taking security for their execution, and by the avoidance of all laxity in enforcing them, the danger may be minimised. From want of attention to these matters loss has been caused to districts in the past, and they will require to be carefully looked after if benefit proportionate to the expenditure is to be derived from new arterial drainage schemes. If Drainage Boards pay due attention to these matters, and support the efforts of the engineers employed by them to secure good work, there is every reason to hope that well considered works of the class under consideration may continue to be beneficially undertaken.

Loans for Improvement of Land.

Nos. 26 and 28 in Abstract, p. 42.

These loans may be divided into two classes :—

1. Loans under the Land Improvement Act, 10 Vic., c. 32, made to owners in fee or of a lesser estate, and to tenants holding under a lease for lives, of which at least two are surviving, or for unexpired terms of not less than 25 years, called "Land Improvement Loans."

2. Loans under Section 31 of the Land Law Act of 1881, made to all tenants save those who hold under a lease for lives or for an unexpired term of 25 years, called "Land Law Loans."

I. *Land Improvement Loans.*

The object of these loans was restricted by the original Act, 10 Vic., c. 32, to drainage, reclamation, subsoiling, fencing, farm-roads, and other field works. Subsequent statutes extended them to the following purposes :—

Works.	Statute.
Building and enlarging Farm-offices, ...	29 & 30 Vic., c. 40, sec. 3
Building and enlarging Farm dwelling-houses, . . .	29 & 30 Vic., c. 40, sec. 4
Building Dwelling-houses for Labourers, . . .	23 & 24 Vic., c. 19, sec. 1
Planting for Shelter, . . .	29 & 30 Vic., c. 40, sec. 5
Erection of Scutch Mills, ...	15 & 16 Vic., c. 34.

The smallest loan permitted was originally £100. The minimum limit has been reduced by statute to £50 for permanent buildings.

Formerly, when a Loan was made to a tenant under the Land Improvement Act, the Board's charge on his land was destroyed by the cesser or determination of the tenancy. This is no longer the case. By the Public Works Loans Act of 1869 (32 & 33 Vic., c. 71, sections 5 & 6), the loan continues after cesser or determination of the lessee's interest to be a charge on the landlord's estate, but only to the extent of the value of the improvement at the time when the lessee's interest came to an end. In case of dispute this value is assessed by the Commissioner of Valuation.

II. *Loans to Tenants under the Land Law Act of* 1881, *or "Land Law Loans."*

These loans are authorised for improvements which experience has shown to be permanently useful for agricultural tenancies of various sizes. At first the minimum was fixed at £100, but this was found to impede advances for small holdings and minor improvements, and successive reductions have brought the minimum to £25, a figure which has been practically found low enough to meet small requirements. In the earlier stages of this service the maximum loan under the Land Law Act was five times the valuation or judicial rent. Defaults in repayment of the advances occurred to an extent which, while not sufficient to throw a doubt on the honesty or general solvency of the borrowing class, was enough to show that a risk existed, against which it was necessary in the public interest to take precautions. Much of the default, and consequently much of the risk, occurred in cases where eviction for non-payment of rent took place, or was probable, the determination of the tenancy operating as an extinguishment of the Board's charge. Under these circumstances it was proposed to extend to Land Law Loans the principle applied by the Public Works Loans Act of 1889 to loans to tenants under the Land Improvement Act, thus making the holding liable after the determination of the tenancy, but only to the extent of the value of the improvement at such determination to be assessed by the Commissioner of Valuation as an independent authority. The assessments of the Valuation Office in cases under the Act of 1889 had been accepted as satisfactory by owners, and it was thought that a system which had been found to work equitably in the ambit in which it had been tested could have been extended without fear of evil consequences, and with the result of securing the State against undue risk of loss, and of limiting the liability placed on the owner's interest carefully limited to the value to him and his representatives of the improvement effected. The proposal not having been adopted, it became necessary to adopt measures in order to diminish the risk against which it had been directed, and in consequence the maximum of loans to tenants under the Land Law Act was reduced from five to three times the valuation or judicial rent. The reduction does not apply in cases where the risk is covered by security collateral to the Board's charge on the tenant's holding, nor where the rent is so small relatively to the value as to remove practically the risk of eviction.

There exists another difference between "Land Improvement" and "Land Law" Loans to which attention may be directed. Under the latter the borrower is placed by a covenant in the mortgage deed under a direct obligation to the Board to maintain the works carried out by the loan. The benefit of this obligation to the borrower as well as to the State is obvious, and the steps taken to enforce it by maintenance inspections are referred to at page 18 of this Report. There is a difficulty in creating it in the Land Improvement Loans, because the instrument of security under that system is not, as in the case of Land Law Loans, a deed with which a covenant to maintain can be incorporated, but a charging order into which such a provision cannot be introduced. The point is one of increasing importance owing to the growing number of loans to purchasers under the Land Commission, which must generally be made under the Land Improvement Act. It is in the interest not only of the borrower and the Board of Works, but also perhaps in a wider sense of the Land Commission, that there should be a well defined and enforceable obligation to maintain in such cases.

The spirit in which this service has been dealt with by applicants and borrowers has been steadily improving. When Land Law Loans were first introduced, there is no doubt that in some instances they were sometimes sought with the intention of using the money for the purchase of stock or the discharge of liabilities rather than for the improvement of the holding. This tendency, never general, was checked at an early stage. As time went on it disappeared through careful supervision and the growing desire of borrowers to use the loans for the real and permanent improvement of the land. This tone prevails among tenant borrowers at the present day and helps to guard against serious abuse of the facilities afforded by the system. Applicants show a tendency to co-operate with the Board in limiting the loan to what is really necessary to meet cash expenditure on works. At first, instalments of loans were issued in anticipation of work. For some years past the order has been changed, and the loan is issued in parts on the gradual execution of the works. This system is carried out in such a manner as to avoid inconvenience or delay to the borrowers, and while it serves the interests of the Board by rendering misappropriation difficult, it serves equally those of the agriculturist by making him active in securing the prompt and satisfactory execution of work on which the advance depends. The expenditure out of tenants' loans on buildings is largely in excess of that on drainage, reclamation, &c. This may be attributed largely to the very defective accommodation to be found in most of the smaller holdings for residence as well as for cattle and the storage of produce. In many, perhaps most instances, the farmer gives priority to the claims of cattle and produce and postpones to them the necessity, often only too evident, of a suitable dwelling house. Applications for loans for drainage are each year more limited to cases where substantial pecuniary advantage is certain to be gained. The tendency to seek aid for works of doubtful benefit is constantly decreasing.

Although Tenant Purchasers generally borrow under the Land Improvement Act, it may be permitted to refer to them in speaking of the class which furnishes borrowers under the Land Law Act. The reports of our Inspectors bear testimony to the desire shown by them to improve their newly purchased holdings. Their anxiety to secure improvements which are productive of profit rather than mere convenience or comfort, their efforts to secure the greatest advantage with the smallest amount of indebtedness to the Board, and their readiness to comply with regulations and requirements made to secure good work, deserve to be noted.

Loans for iron-roofed hay barns are becoming very general in most parts of the country. When introduced it was believed that they would not only prove a convenience but also add substantially to the value of the hay crop. This anticipation has been fully realised, and the growing demand for these structures is the consequence. It has been found necessary to be strict in framing and enforcing requirements for their careful construction. Borrowers and contractors are sometimes surprised at the care with which the materials supplied and the work done under these loans are watched, but it is certain that only such vigilance could secure iron hay barns able to resist the wear and tear of twenty-two years (the period of currency of the loan), or such violent storms as prevailed in the beginning of this year.

Disappointment is occasionally felt by applicants under the Land Improvement and Land Law Acts at some of the conditions and restrictions attached to the Board's loans. Many of these conditions and restrictions are imposed by statute, all are it is believed necessary for one or both of the two objects which it is the duty of the Board to serve, the safety of the State in making the loan and the permanent and real improvement of the lands. We venture to instance one case of common occurrence. A farmer has two holdings A and B, of say thirty acres each at distinct judicial rents, and at such a distance from each other as to be virtually unmanageable as one holding. He seeks a loan to build out-offices on A large enough to serve the requirements of both farms at a cost necessitating a loan which would possibly exceed the amount for which a charge on A would be sufficient security. To comply with this application would be to provide A with a building considerably in excess of its wants, and, to the extent of the excess, no real improvement to it, but rather a burden, inasmuch as it imposes on the farm a larger indebtedness and rentcharge and a heavier maintenance expenditure than necessary. It may be said that these burdens could be lightened by charging B as well as A with the loan. But B may be sold by the applicant, or the two farms may pass in many ways into different hands, and there would follow the very undesirable result of leaving B charged with a debt contracted for an improvement of no possible use to it, situated on another farm. The evil is felt particularly when the tenant of A, and still more when the tenant of B, seeks to purchase under the Land Commission. The former is naturally met with the difficulty that he is burdened with a rentcharge for repayment of an expenditure for which his holding has not got adequate value, and the latter that his holding is liable for a debt for works which are productive of no value whatever to it under existing circumstances. It will be seen that the Board are bound to give effect to these considerations, but in doing so they weigh the circumstances of each case and consult the convenience of parties so far as consistent with prudence and legality.

The "Maintenance Inspections" which have been proceeding for the last two years have proved of service, and it is proposed to continue them. The condition which they disclose may be regarded on the whole as not unsatisfactory. In some instances improvements effected under the older loans had been seriously neglected, but, with these exceptions, works have, as a rule, been fairly maintained. Repairs of various kinds are no doubt frequently found necessary. The Board's requirements are in almost all cases speedily complied with, and the slight expense or trouble incurred is amply repaid by the preservation of the improvement from further decay. We desire to bear testimony to the spirit in which these inspections have been met. Borrowers and the present occupiers of holdings on which loans have been made have co-operated cheerfully with the Inspectors, and appear pleased at receiving guidance for repair and preservation. It has also been found that in many districts their neighbours, on seeing repairs effected on the holdings visited, set to work without formal inspection to put the improvements on their own farms into good order.

We have found it necessary during the year, as occasionally in former periods, to decline applications for loans from local authorities and individuals where the payments on previous loans made to applicants were in arrear. From the circumstance that in some instances re-application after refusal has been made while arrears were still due, it is feared that the position of the Board on this point is not universally understood. We endeavour in such cases to make it clear that the statutory powers under which loans are made do not abrogate the responsibility which lies on the Board quite as much as on other institutions entrusted with money to be lent, and that the existence of arrears, or serious irregularity in the repayment of previous advances, renders it impossible for the Board to recommend applications for new loans for your Lordships' sanction.

With regard to the whole Loans Service, the following table shows the payments, and the arrears of principal and interest for the last four years :—

—	Payments.	Arrears.		
		Principal.	Interest.	Total.
	£	£	£	£
1891–92, . .	652,937	318,497	298,873	631,370
1892–93, . .	783,061	346,631	201,743	648,374
1893–94, . .	767,241	346,857	183,030	561,887
1894–95, . .	783,374	367,469	205,390	572,859

The following Abstract shows the Services on which these arrears occur :—

—	31st March, 1892.	31st March, 1893.	31st March, 1894.	31st March, 1895.
	£	£	£	£
Public Works Loans generally, . .	60,147	50,820	53,824	60,603
Clare Bog Reclamation Loan, . .	38,317	—	—	—
Public Health Act, ...	2,458	2,068	2,029	1,496
Railways, ...	385,786	404,124	430,593	441,181
Land Charges, payable by Owners, .	70,081	85,620	61,729	59,509
Do., do. Occupiers, .	7,785	10,053	10,026	12,384
Seed supply, ...	16,329	15,706	24,664	14,571
	631,370	648,374	561,887	572,859

The total amount of arrears in the Accountant's books has increased by £10,972 from £561,887 (1894) to £572,859 on 31st March, 1895. To arrive at the true increase, the arrears included in the amount written off from the Local Loans Fund by the Public Works Loans Act of 1894 must be added. That amount was £79, made up of principal and interest arrears. The total arrears therefore on the 31st March, 1895, would, but for the operation of the Public Works Loans Act, 1891, have stood at £572,938. Eliminating, however, the increase on certain railway loans (£14,596), which cannot be arrested, the work of recovering arrears during the year may fairly be regarded as satisfactory.

Arrears on "Public Works Loans generally" show an increase of £6,779, which is accounted for by the non-payment of the annual principal instalment on the Newry Navigation Loan (the result of agreement by which the money goes to discharge a salvage loan of £15,000 made in 1890), and by increased arrears on some of the Harbour Loans, which, in consequence of former reports, it is perhaps unnecessary to refer to in detail. The only new features contributing to the increase are suspensions of the principal repayments on the loans of two harbours, which have been permitted by your Lordships under special circumstances.

Public Health Act arrears have been reduced from £2,029 to £1,496. This is so far satisfactory, but we look forward to a time when, except in case of overwhelming local distress, local authorities will universally recognise the necessity of raising sufficient rates for the discharge of their liabilities to the State, and applying the moneys collected to that purpose.

The arrears on Seed Supply Loans under the Act of 1880 stood at £12,037 at the commencement of the year, and have not been decreased. Those under the Act of 1890 have decreased from £13,627 to £2,517.

We are glad to report a continued progress in the recovery of Land Improvement Charges, the decrease in arrears effected in the year being £2,120.

On the other hand, arrears on Loans to Tenants under Section 31 of the Land Law Act show an increase of £2,359 14s. 8d. We have already referred to the risks in connection with this service, and, while we have no desire to exaggerate them, it must be admitted that they deserve serious attention. It is true that a large part of the existing arrears have arisen in a few localities, and that the evil in its worst form cannot be said to be general; that delay in payment does not necessarily mean ultimate loss, and that the increase during the past year is to some extent mere unpunctuality due to a bad season. But, making every allowance, two inferences appear inevitable:—First that it is our duty to make every reasonable effort to prevent the growth of fresh cases of arrear, and, where arrears exist, to effect recovery, immediate when practicable, and under other circumstances gradual; second, that in making loans it is important to be thoroughly assured that the borrower is fairly able to meet his ordinary liabilities, and that his farm, whether large or small, is stocked or provided with means of cultivation; in other words, that he has sufficient capital or its equivalent to carry on the ordinary work of farming without loss. The Board have always inquired into these points, but the necessity for attention to them is obviously increasing. Apart from our primary duty to the State to avoid unsafe loans, we cannot but feel that to lend to a tenant whose circumstances render repayment difficult or impossible, is a doubtful benefit.

There exists on some estates a tendency to create what is known as a "hanging gale" on the Board's charges. This means that the rent-charge should be habitually six months in arrear, that the April gale should be paid in October, and the October gale in the following April, and that this system should be recognised and have the force of a custom. The experience of the Board is that in many instances delay in paying one gale leads to suspension of further payments. Apart from this it is unnecessary to point out that the terms on which advances are made are fixed on the assumption of punctuality, and cannot be violated without risk of loss to the Local Loans Fund. It has been said that the efforts made by the Board to ensure punctuality necessitates pressure on tenants. The cases which have come under notice are such as can be met without such pressure. The real difficulty is caused by accumulated arrears of instalments, by payments to puisne incumbrancers, and even to owners, of sums which should be retained to meet payments to the Board on the point of accruing due. Receivers under the Landed Estates Court would be obliged to make provision for all fixed and ascertained liabilities under such circumstances, and it has not been found that their action has created a necessity for pressure on the tenants whose rents they collect. The endeavours of the Board have been gradual, and have given ample opportunity to make arrangements for the restoration of regularity without sudden cessation of payments to incumbrancers or owners, and without any necessity for pressure on tenants. All that is wanted is a fair observance of priorities, and it is felt that if this be adopted, agents will be relieved from the anxiety expressed in the isolated instances referred to.

In the course of the year, five railway Loans have been paid off, viz.:—

	£
Donegal Railway,	13,000
West Donegal (now Donegal),	40,000
Clonakilty Extension,	20,000
Bann Valley,	40,000
West Clare,	64,400

The last mentioned loan was secured on Baronial Guaranteed Shares.

The Clara and Banagher Railway has been sold to the Great Southern and Western Railway Company for £5,000. The Board has lent for the construction of this line £60,000, of which £30,000 was charged on the undertaking alone, and £30,000 on baronial cess as well as on the undertaking. Similarly, the Draperstown Railway, on which there was an outstanding principal debt to the Board of £16,000, has been sold for £2,000 to the Belfast and Northern Counties Railway Company. Bills authorising both transfers have received the Royal Assent.

Taking advantage of the favourable state of the money market, the Pembroke Township Commissioners (Dublin) have issued Stock, and paid off the outstanding balance, amounting to £38,600, of the loans made by this Department. Similar arrangements were made during the financial year, and have been carried out since its close by Belfast and Kingstown. The Lurgan Town Commissioners are taking steps in the same direction.

V.—LEGISLATION IN 1894-95 AFFECTING SERVICES ADMINISTERED BY THE BOARD.

By the 4th Section of the Public Works Loan Act, 1894 (57 Vic., c. 11), annuities payable to the Land Commission were given priority in all cases over Loans by the Board to tenants under Sec. 31 of the Land Law Act, and under certain circumstances over Loans made by the Board under the Land Improvement Act.

By the Seed Potatoes Supply (Ireland) Act, 1895 (58 Vic., c. 2), the Board were empowered to make advances to Poor Law Unions for the purchase of seed potatoes to be supplied to occupiers who are unable to procure an adequate supply of same

The amount so advanced up to the 31st March last was £21,937, and the further sum since advanced is £38,449, making a total of £60,886 to date.

These advances are to be repaid in two instalments—the first on the 1st August, 1894, and the second on the following 1st August. They are subject to interest at 3½ per cent. per annum, which is to be discharged out of the Irish Church Fund.

It will be remembered that, in 1893, an agreement was made for the sale to the Fishguard Bay Railway and Pier Company, Limited, of the Waterford and Wexford Railway, connecting Wexford with Rosslare, and of Rosslare Harbour. Amongst other conditions imposed on the purchasers were the obligation to repair the Railway and the works at the Harbour. The Railway was put in order and opened for traffic during the course of the year, and repairs are in progress at the Harbour, which has been found useful for the purposes of traffic within the period under report. A Bill vesting the Railway and Harbour in the purchasing Company received the Royal Assent on the 1st July, 1894.

The tolls and dues of the Shannon Navigation have within the year been brought under the operation of the Railway and Canal Traffic Act, 1888. In 1839, by 2 & 3 Vict., c. 61, a classification of goods was established and certain maximum charges permitted. These maximum charges were not fully enforced, but a schedule of tolls at lower rates was adopted. To any alteration of this schedule the consent of the Treasury was necessary under the Statute last referred to, and although formal steps towards an increase were taken on one occasion, your Lordships finally decided that the then actual rates or "actuals" should remain undisturbed. In this state of things, the Board of Trade, in 1893, in exercise of its functions under the Railway and Canal Traffic Act of 1888, having called on us to frame a classification of traffic and schedule of maximum rates, we proceeded to comply, adopting the classification of traffic generally in use under the Act of 1888, and proposing a schedule of rates as nearly equivalent in its working to the maximum tolls and dues under the 2 & 3 Vic., c. 61, as the differences between the old and new classifications would permit. The Board of Trade, following the course generally adopted with regard to owners of waterways and railways and to carrying companies, substituted for the proposed schedule framed on the old maximum rates a schedule framed on the Board's "actuals." It was pointed out by the Board of Works that they collected tolls, &c., not for purposes of dividend or profit in any sense, but only with the object of providing for the maintenance of the Navigation, and that if "actuals" (with the other sources of available revenue) at any time proved insufficient for the latter purpose, the deficit would be thrown on the votes of Parliament, or the Navigation allowed to fall into disrepair and disuse. The question was ultimately settled by 57 & 58 Vict., ch. ccvi., by which, after full inquiry before a Committee of both Houses, a schedule was adopted which (1) fixed maximum tolls at a reduced but still sufficient margin over "actuals," (2) secured the Board its existing actuals, and (3) provided that the "actuals" as they stood at the passing of the Act shall not be raised without the assent of the Treasury to be communicated to the Houses of Parliament.

We have the honour to be

Your Lordships' obedient Servants,

R. H. SANKEY.

R. O'SHAUGHNESSY.

G. A. STEVENSON.

P. J. Tuohy, *Secretary.*

29th *June*, 1895.

APPENDICES.

General Statement as to the Duties of the Board.

The general scope of these duties may be gathered from the following extract from the Report of the Committee appointed in 1870 to inquire into the administration by the Board of the services with which it is charged:—

> "The variety of these services is very great. The Commissioners not only conduct all the business which is delegated to two separate Boards in London (namely, the Commissioners of Her Majesty's Works and Public Buildings, and the Public Works Loan Commissioners), and part of that which is intrusted to the Inclosure Commissioners (9 & 10 Vic., c. 101), but they also have under their charge a considerable amount of work which is not done in Great Britain at all by the Government, such as the maintenance of Inland Navigations, &c.; they are likewise members of the Board of Control for Lunatic Asylums, and of the Board of Control over the Royal Canal.
>
> "To be charged with the lending of sums of public money is, of itself, a trust, the importance of which it is not easy to overrate; and when to this is added the control of an expenditure of over £300,000 a year; the care of a large amount of valuable public property; the interpretation and administration of very numerous Acts of Parliament; and the conduct of much extraneous business, some idea may be formed of the responsibilities thrown on this Board.
>
> "Moreover, the Board of Works occupies a position peculiar to itself. It is the only Department of the State which has under its charge loan operations as well as a large expenditure. In having to accommodate local authorities and individuals with capital, which they cannot so cheaply raise in the open market, and at the same time keep watch over a public expenditure, the Board has more or less conflicting interests to deal with; it has to consult the special interests of localities and persons and at the same time to protect the general interests of the public. Its duties, therefore, may at times be attended with more than ordinary difficulties."

Since the date of that report the duties of the Board have been largely increased both by automatic development and as the result of legislation.

We may particularly refer to the loans authorised by the 31st Section of the Land Law (Ireland) Act, 1881, under which £890,697 in 10,835 separate amounts has been advanced, the Sea Fisheries Ireland Act, 1883, the Ancient Monuments Acts, the numerous amendments and extensions of our powers to lend for local and educational purposes, and the important duties imposed upon us in connection with the schemes of railway extension promoted under the Tramways and Public Companies (Ireland) Act, 1883, and the Light Railways (Ireland) Act, 1889.

Within the same period the duties of the Board have only been reduced by a reconstitution of the Board of Control, of which only the Chairman is now a member, though the whole clerical, accounting, draughtsman's, and legal work is carried on by our staff, and by the transfer to the Congested Districts Board of the Sea Coast and Fisheries Fund and of the Irish Reproductive Loan Fund, with the exception of £20,000 which remains under our control.

In the Session of 1892 several Acts were passed affecting the status of the Board and their loan services.

By the Public Works Loans Act, 1892 (55 and 56 Vict., cap. 61, section 8), the Commissioners were incorporated for all the various duties they discharge with perpetual succession, and a common seal, with power to hold land, and such incorporation is thereby made retrospective as regards previous contracts or securities.

By the Ancient Monuments Protection Act, 1892 (55 and 56 Vict., cap. 46), the Ancient Monuments Protection Act, of 1882, has been extended, and by such extension the Commissioners have already become guardians of, and are thus enabled to protect and preserve monuments of historic and artistic interest which would otherwise be liable to be destroyed or become ruinous.

By the Drainage and Improvement of Lands (Ireland) Act, 1892 (55 and 56 Vict., cap. 65), tenants by agreement with their landlords or by order of the Board can promote and carry out Schemes for Arterial Drainage, under the Arterial Drainage Act of 1863, and the Acts amending and extending same.

By the same Acts, Sec. 11, we were given power to apportion charges for Drainage Maintenance on portions of lands liable to such a charge.

The Seed Potatoes (Ireland) Act, 1895 (58 Vic., c. 2) permitted the Board during the Spring of 1895 to make advances to Poor Law Unions for the purchase of Seed Potatoes.

APPENDIX (A).

Details of Voted Services.

Public Buildings.

Queen's Colleges.—New workshops and stores have been completed at Cork, and, after consultation with the College authorities and settlement of plans, tenders have been received for the new Physiological and Pathological Laboratories at Belfast.

Royal University.—The Physical Laboratory has been completed.

Dundrum Central Criminal Lunatic Asylum.—See General Observations, p. 6.

Royal Irish Constabulary Buildings.—Contracts have been signed for the erection of a new barrack for fifty-five men, including a head constable's quarters, at Springfield-road, Belfast, and for new stabling for twenty-eight horses at the Central Barrack, Musgrave-street, Belfast, and considerable progress has been made with the former. Important sanitary works at Ennis Barrack, and improvements in the quarters of the Constable of the Troop, and in the Dining Room of No. 2 Company at the Depôt in the Phœnix Park have been carried out.

Science and Art Buildings.—The Natural History Museum has been lit by electricity, and the area at the back of the Museum has been extended to admit of proper boiler drainage. A new oak staircase has been erected in the Art Museum to give access from the ground-floor to the Royal Irish Academy collection in the basement. New girders and flooring have been supplied and fixed on the principal floor of the School of Art, and a new Waiting Room has been erected at the Botanic Gardens at Glasnevin.

Royal Dublin Society.—The building of New Lecture Theatre is progressing. It will occupy the space lying between Leinster House, the Art Museum, and the Natural History Museum, hitherto occupied by the Old Lecture Theatre and the laboratory, &c., of the Royal Dublin Society.

High Courts of Justice.—Considerable progress has been made with the new Bar Library, and the consequent alterations in the adjoining offices and courts. The two upper floors of the building at the rere of the eastern courtyard have been cleared out; accommodation for the several offices displaced have been found elsewhere in the building, and the new library, waiting-rooms, &c., are being constructed in the space thus rendered available.

The re-fitting of the Court of Exchequer has been completed.

Royal Hospital.—The fire mains have been extended, and some new hydrants fixed.

Chief Secretary's Offices, &c.—The Under Secretary's residence, Dublin Castle, has been adapted for use as offices, and is now partially occupied. Several sanitary improvements have been carried out, and a room fitted-up for microscopic work at the Veterinary Department. The chief messenger's quarters in the basement of the Chief Secretary's Offices have been enlarged and improved.

Dublin Metropolitan Police.—The projected improvements of Green-street Courthouse have been carried out by the Dublin Corporation, and the Parliamentary grant in aid (£1,000) paid. The erection of the new barrack at Chapelizod is progressing. Improvements have been carried out in the cells at the Central Police Courts, and at the mess-room of the Detective Division. Several minor works of sanitation have been carried out at the Dublin barracks and stations.

National Education Buildings.—An iron hay shed, and boar and poultry houses have been completed, and a pumping engine erected at the Munster Model Farm.

Revenue Buildings.—The whole of the basements of the Dublin Customs and Inland Revenue buildings have been concreted.

Coast Guard Stations.—New stations have been completed at Waterville, County Kerry, and at Bunowen and Bunbeg, County Galway, the latter including a divisional officer's residence. The two latter are already, and the former will soon be in occupation. Contracts for the erection of a new station at Union Hall, near Skibbereen, County Cork, and of a boat house and divisional carpenter's workshop at Rathmullen have been signed.

Royal Naval Reserve Stations.—A new firing battery and drill shed have been completed at Larne, and handed over to the Admiralty, and the buildings for the drill instructor and crew at Galway Battery are approaching completion.

State Residences.—A considerable portion of the boundary wall of the Private Secretary's Lodge has been re-built. A new plant house has been erected at the Chief Secretary's Lodge, Phœnix Park, and the heating apparatus of two others renewed. One of the main chimney stacks in the State Apartments, Dublin Castle, has been re-built, and St. Patrick's Hall has been freshly decorated.

Postal and Telegraph Buildings.—With regard to the new Parcels Post Depot, Amiens-street, see General Observations, page 6.

The new post office and post master's residence at Wexford, and the alterations, additions, and new fittings at King-street Post Office, Waterford, have been completed. The Telegraph Stores at Cork are complete and in occupation.

Irish Land Commission Offices.—The raising of the Record building was virtually completed, a storey very similar in construction to the new strong-room at the General Registry Office having been added to the existing building.

Ordnance Survey Office.—The Warrant Officers' Quarters have been completed.

General Register Office.—The new strong-room and offices in connection are virtually completed, and were occupied in May. The buildings consist of an extensive two-storey strong-room, fitted up with steel racks, and a commodious office approached by a separate entrance from Rutland-square. The construction is fireproof throughout, and the windows and roof lights of the strong-room are provided with steel shutters opened and closed simultaneously by suitable gearing.

Public Gardens, &c.

The Phœnix Park and St. Stephen's-Green Park, Dublin, and the Curragh of Kildare.—The usual works of maintenance and repair in connection with the buildings, roads, grounds, planting, &c., have been carried out. With reference to the Phœnix Park, see p. 7, General Observations.

Depositories for Parochial Records Act, 39 and 40 Vic., c. 58.—Under the provisions of this Act, inspections of proposed depositories have been made in eight cases, and reports thereon forwarded to the Deputy Keeper of Records.

National Education, Grants in Aid of Erecting and Improving National Schools.—See General Observations, p. 7.

ROYAL HARBOURS.

A Summary of Rainfall and Tidal Observations at Kingstown, and remarks by the Harbour Masters on the Fishing Industry and Trade at the several Harbours, will be found in Appendix (G).

Kingstown Harbour, Co. Dublin.

New dredging plant was delivered during the latter portion of the year, and a quantity of 27,000 tons was lifted from the harbour bed and deposited at sea. The breakwater, piers, slips, wharves, roads and buildings were kept in repair, and a commencement was made with the erection of a larger shed on the Mail Packet Pier for the better accommodation of the mail and passenger traffic, and it will be finished early in current year.

Her Majesty's ships, the vessels of the Irish Lights Board and trading vessels were supplied with water, and ballast was also supplied to the latter.

Howth, Dunmore East, Donaghadee, and Ardglass Harbours.

These harbours have been duly maintained. Dunmore and Donaghadee have suffered slightly, and Ardglass severely, from the winter storms. In the last mentioned a mass of concrete, 34 tons in weight, was torn and lifted away from the toe of the sea slope in one solid block. At Dunmore and Donaghadee the necessary repairs have been executed. At Ardglass they are in progress. The berthage at the south dock of this harbour has been considerably improved.

SHANNON DRAINAGE.

The remaining dams at Killaloe were removed, and the drainage works at that point of the river thus completed.

The floors of the sluices at Killaloe and Athlone were strengthened and protected, and the sluices and other works connected with the drainage maintained in good order.

RIVER MAIGUE NAVIGATION.

The hand rail of swivel bridge was raised and the Collector's house and the bridge maintained.

LOWER BOYNE NAVIGATION.

New deep gates were put in at Rossnaree Lock and the works generally were maintained in good order. This was done before the completion of arrangements for the transfer of the navigation to the Boyne Navigation Company, referred to at p. 8.

APPENDIX (B.)

Details of Non-Voted Services.

Arterial Drainage and Improvement of Lands (Ireland) Act, 1863, and Amendments.

26 & 27 Vic., c. 88; 27 & 28 Vic., c. 72; 28 & 29 Vic., c. 52; 32 & 33 Vic., c. 72; 35 & 36 Vic., c. 31; 37 & 38 Vic., c. 32; 41 & 42 Vic., c. 59; and 43 & 44 Vic., c. 27; and 55 & 56 Vic., c. 65.

The total number of applications received from the passing of the first of these Acts in the year 1863 to the 31st of March, 1895, is 93.

The maps, plans, estimates, and valuation schedules have been deposited, together with petitions for the constitution of the Bunkey Drainage District in the counties of Limerick and Tipperary.

An order for substitution of tenants for landlords as proprietors was made under 55 & 56 Victoria, c. 65, in the case of the Carrigrohane (co. Cork) scheme, and the district was duly constituted.

The works in the River Suck District (counties Galway and Roscommon) have been completed (see pages 11 and 12), and the final award has been made in the Killard District, county Cork.

A schedule of the final awards made under these Acts will be found in the Appendix, (D 6), pages 64–69.

D 2

NON-VOTED SERVICES—*continued.*

The total area of land drained or improved in the 56 districts in which final awards have been made, is 111,269 statute acres, and the total cost chargeable thereto amounts to £874,716. This has been in addition to the works of the 121 districts carried out under the Act 5 & 6 Vic., c. 89, and the Acts amending it, between the years 1842 and 1860, on which an expenditure of £2,390,619 was incurred, of which £158,180 was for works chargeable on counties; £141,073 a free grant; £1,207,382 remitted; and £883,777 made repayable by annuity or otherwise; a total of 266,736 acres was drained or improved under the latter Act.

INCREASED RENTS IN RESPECT OF ARTERIAL DRAINAGE RENT CHARGES.

No applications to fix increased rents in respect of improvements were received by the Board during the year.

DRAINAGE MAINTENANCE, 29 AND 30 VIC., c. 49.

No cases of maintenance under this Act arose during the year.

MAINTENANCE OF NAVIGATIONS WORKS.

19 and 20 Vic., c. 62.

No works have been carried out under this Act during the year.

RAILWAY CLAUSES CONSOLIDATION ACT.

8 Vic., c. 20, sec. 23.

No certificate was issued during the year.

FISHERY PIERS AND HARBOURS MAINTENANCE.

16 & 17 Vic., c. 136.

The damage done to Malin Head Pier, County Donegal, by winter storms has been made good at a cost of £440. The wharf wall at Carlingford Pier, County Louth, has been strengthened at a cost of £708. Damage having occurred to the Pier at Kilkeel, County Down, the necessary repairs have been commenced. Storm damages at Buncrana Pier, County Donegal, were also commenced, and are in progress. The damage at Boat Strand, County Waterford, mentioned in last report, has been dealt with by the County Authority.

SEA FISHERIES (IRELAND) ACT, 1883.

The works at Greystones Harbour received attention, and some further work will be necessary in the present year before handing it over to the County.

ARKLOW HARBOUR.

The North Groyne Works undertaken by the Harbour Commissioners, for which a grant of £3,500 and a loan of £3,500 were sanctioned, have been completed.

SHANNON NAVIGATION.

The lock-gates at Roosky and the breast-gates at Albert Lock have been renewed. The locks, towpaths, bridges, roads, buoys, &c., were (where necessary) repaired and kept in good order.

NATIONAL MONUMENTS AND ECCLESIASTICAL RUINS.

(See p. 30.)

Post Roads.

Act 6 and 7 Wm. IV., cap. 116, section 61.

Applications from the Postmaster-General were received during the past year for repairs of Post Roads situate in the following counties:—

County Tipperary—Cahir to Ardfinnan.
County Waterford—Youghal Bridge to Clashmore.
County Waterford—Borough Bounds at Waterford to County Bounds at Granagh.
County Down—Lisburn to Ballynahinch.

In these cases, with the exception of the last, which the Board were advised did not come within the provisions of the Act 16 & 17 Vic., c. 136, the repairs were executed under the superintendence of the respective County Surveyors from funds supplied by the Board, to be repaid by levy placed on the respective counties.

County Surveyors' Assistants.

Nine candidates for the office of County Surveyors' Assistant have been examined under Warrant of the Lord Lieutenant, pursuant to the provisions of the Act 6 & 7 Wm. IV., cap. 116, and the qualifications of seven certified to the respective County Surveyors.

Limited Owners Residences (Settled Estates Acts).

27 & 28 Vic., c. 113; 33 & 34 Vic., c. 56; 34 & 35 Vic., c. 84; 40 & 41 Vic., c. 31.

Three applications have been made under these Acts during past year.

Arbitrations under "The Railways (Ireland) Acts,"

(1851, 1860, 1864),

14 & 15 Vic., c. 70; 23 & 24 Vic., c. 97; and 27 & 28 Vic., c. 71.

Arbitrations have been applied for and Arbitrators appointed in the following cases, viz.:—

Railway Companies:

The Great Northern Railway—Lands required under the Great Northern Railway (Ireland) Act, 1891.
The Great Northern Railway—To assess value of minerals at Coalisland.
Dublin, Wicklow, and Wexford Railway—Lands required in connection with the Loop Line.
Midland Great Western Railway—Additional land.
Achill Extension Railway—Lands required in connection with the Achill Extension Railway Order, 1894.

Town Commissioners:

Lisburn—Lands required for Lisburn Waterworks.
Clones—Lands required for Clones Waterworks.
Rathmines—Lands required for Rathmines Waterworks.
Kingstown—Lands required for Cholera Hospital.
Pembroke—Lands required in connection with the Local Government Board Provisional Orders Confirmation (No. 13) Act, 1894.

Corporations:

Dublin—Widening of John's-lane.
Belfast—Lands required in connection with the Local Government Board (Ireland) Provisional Orders Confirmation (No. 13) Act, 1891.

Boards of Guardians of Poor Law Unions:

Ballymena, Baltinglass, Borrisokane, Cashel, Dundalk (2), Dungarvan, Edenderry, Ennis, Limerick, Mallow, Mountmellick, Mullingar, Navan, North Dublin, Youghal.	For the purposes of the Labourers (Ireland) Acts.
Coleraine, Strabane, Waterford,	For Waterworks.

Trustees requiring Land for Teachers' Residences and Schools:

The Trustees Cornabarrile National School.
" Tobergal "
" Callystown "

Other Applicants:

Blackrock and Kingstown Main Drainage Board—Land required for the Main Drainage Scheme.
Grand Jury of the County Kilkenny—In connection with Mountgarrett Bridge.
Belfast Water Commissioners—Belfast Water Works.
The Secretary of State for War—Lands required under (1) Ranges Act, 1891, and (2) Defence Acts.
Tralee Urban Sanitary Authority—New road in Tralee.

APPENDIX C.

DETAILS OF LOAN SERVICES, WITH ABSTRACT OF ACCOUNTS AND TABLES.

Class I.—Loans secured on Undertakings.

Labourers' Dwellings in Towns and Housing of the Working Classes.
Nos. 7 and 8 in Abstract, p. 40.

Labouring Classes Dwellings (Ireland) Act, 1866 (29 & 30 Vic., c. 44); and the Housing of the Working Classes Acts, 1885, 1890, and 1893 (48 & 49 Vic., c. 72, and 53 and 54 Vic., c. 70).

Amount of loans sanctioned under Act of 1866, while it continued operative, i.e., to the close of the year 1884-85—£281,384. Number of dwellings erected—3,416. Rate of Interest charged—4 per cent.

In previous reports we called attention to the stimulus to building under this service, arising from the favourable terms as to interest granted by Treasury Minutes of 21st and 25th January, 1883. During the past year 9 applications to the amount of £36,209 have been sanctioned, as against 7 for £11,463 in 1893-94.

The following table shows the number and amount of the loans made each year during the periods referred to.

Year.		No. of applications sanctioned.	Amount sanctioned.		No. of families to be accommodated.
			£	s.	
1866-67,	.	Nil	..		Nil.
1867-68,	.	1	438	0	8
1868-69,	.	Nil	—		Nil.
1869-70,	.	1	600	0	10
1870-71,	.	1	4,146	0	138
1871-72,	.	1	1,680	0	46
1872-73,	.	3	7,175	0	108
1873-74,	.	7	32,290	0	281
1874-75,	.	1	910	0	12
1875-76,	.	7	24,242	0	659
1876-77,	.	6	11,100	0	183
1877-78,	.	8	23,614	0	873
1878-79,	.	10	7,100	0	61
1879-80,	.	19	31,838	0	351
1880-81,	.	17	28,870	0	323
1881-82,	.	17	33,674	0	653
1882-83,	.	18	21,167	0	270
1883-84,	.	16	40,052	0	397
1884-85,	.	19	23,364	0	838
1885-86,	.	20	30,785	0	713
1886-87,	.	24	79,161	0	853
1887-88,	.	20	34,756	10	397
1888-89,	.	38	63,765	10	873
1889-90,	.	18	46,319	0	603
1890-91,	.	20	63,413	0	628
1891-92,	.	11	10,164	0	135
1892-93,	.	8	61,370	0	481
1893-94,	.	7	17,443	0	88
1894-95,	.	9	34,309	0	183
Total,	.	303	691,580	0	8,036

CLASS (2).—LOANS SECURED ON RATES.

Both the number and the amount of loans sanctioned under this head show an increase.

—	1893-4.	1894-5.
Number of Loans, . .	347	393
Amount of Loans, . .	£419,884	£483,879

Loans for Works carried out by Grand Juries. No. 9 in Abstract, p. 40.

Loans, for works carried out by Grand Juries, show only £1,393 sanctioned in 1894-95 as against £8,840 in 1893-94.

Loans for Public Libraries, Reformatories, and Industrial Schools. No. 11 in Abstract, p. 40.

No loan has been sanctioned for any of these objects.

Loans for Lunatic Asylum Buildings. No. 17 in Abstract, p. 40.

This service shows substantial work both in number and amount of loans sanctioned viz., 16 loans for £97,035 in 1893-4.

Loans under the Public Health Act. Nos. 19 and 37 in Abstract, pp. 40 and 42.

Loans under the Public Health Act of 1878 reached in number 52, and amounted to £153,908, as against the corresponding figures 65 and £164,786 for the previous year. The following table contrasts the two years in detail, and shows some of the many undertakings comprised under the title of "Sanitary Loans."

PURPOSES.	1893–94.		1894–95.	
	Number of Loans.	Amount.	Number of Loans.	Amount.
		£		£
Water Works,	24	68,726	20	55,970
Sewerage,	19	19,301	8	18,808
Burial Grounds,	6	4,700	4	1,350
Paving and Footpaths,	9	46,559	7	41,760
Buildings,	4	4,250	6	8,809
Gas Works and Public Lighting,	3	15,000	5	38,519
Markets,	1	3,600	–	–
Streets,	–	–	2	2,600
	65	£164,786	52	£153,908

The total amount of Loans authorised for Sanitary purposes stood at £2,312,660 on 31st March, 1895, and the total amount issued at £2,256,290.

The distribution of the sum authorised between different sanitary purposes is as follows:—

	£
Water Works	1,091,069
Sewerage,	870,195
Streets (Paving, &c.),	170,899
Public Baths,	16,350
Scavenging,	23,175
Buildings, Gas Works, Cemeteries, Parks, &c.,	532,482
	£2,312,660

Loans under Labourers Acts. No. 21 in Abstract, p. 40.

Loans under the Labourers Acts, 1883 and 1885, show a marked increase on the amounts of the preceding years. The sanctions from the commencement of the service are stated below.

	£
1884–88,	820,996
1888–89,	168,742
1889–90,	89,681
1890–91,	306,427
1891–92,	90,426
1892–93,	117,925
1893–94,	65,390
1894–95,	194,183

The loans sanctioned under these Acts amounted at the end of the year under report to £1,613,856. Ninety-seven out of 159 Unions had borrowed this sum; the remaining Unions had not up to that date availed themselves of the powers given by the Acts. The number of Unions which had borrowed, with the amount sanctioned in each Province, appears from the following figures:—

		£
Munster,	44 Unions,	921,333
Leinster,	38 "	667,951
Connaught,	9 "	12,194
Ulster,	6 "	12,315
	97	£1,613,856

The advances under the Acts in 1894–95 amounted to £89,875, bringing the total advanced to £1,526,157.

Loans for Dispensary Houses. No. 23 in Abstract, p. 40.

Six applications for loans for the construction, &c., of Dispensary Houses have been received, amounting to £8,400. Twelve Loans have been sanctioned in the year, amounting to £12,250; some of these Loans had been applied for before the commencement of the year 1894-5.

CLASS (3).—LOANS SECURED ON LANDS.

This class comprises, in addition to loans made to tenants for purchase of their holdings, in accordance with the provisions of the Land Act of 1870 (under which no advances are now made), the following loans, having for their object the improvement of land:—

(a.) Loans for arterial drainage under 5 & 6 Vic., c. 89.

(b.) Loans made for arterial drainage works (26 & 27 Vic., c. 88), and loans made for the maintenance of such works (29 & 30 Vic., c. 49).

(c.) Loans to "owners" of lands for improvements, under 10 Vic., c. 32, and amending Acts, and under sec. 19 of 44 & 45 Vic., c. 49.

(d.) Loans to occupiers of lands for improvements, under sec. 31 of the Land Law Act, 1881, 44 & 45 Vic., c. 49.

Loans for Arterial Drainage. Nos. 23, 24, and 42 in Abstract, pp. 40 and 42.

From 1842 to 1863 loans for Arterial Drainage were made under 5 and 6 Vic., c. 89. £2,082,052 was lent under this statute, the greater part during and after the famine of 1846. Of this amount £1,207,582 was remitted, and £874,070 principal repaid. The principal still repayable amounts to £393.

From 1863 loans for this purpose have been made under the Drainage and Improvement of Lands Act (Ireland), 1863, 26 and 27 Vic., c. 88, and amending Acts, and since that date the entire amount of loans made under 26 and 27 Vic., c. 88, up to March 31, 1895, is £831,609, including £6,156 lent out of the Irish Church Fund.

Loans for Land Improvement. No. 20 in Abstract, p. 42.

We submit the numbers of applications for loans, and the amounts issued in each year from 1847, when this service commenced, to 31st March, 1895:—

—	No. of Applications.	Amounts Issued.	—	No. of Applications.	Amounts Issued.
1847, June to Dec. (inclusive),	1,334	672,790	1872-73,	223	416,290
1848,	571	236,160	1873-74,	224	99,378
1849,	643	379,836	1874-75,	243	102,463
1850,	436	230,371	1875-76,	263	94,13[illegible]
1851,	260	143,633	1876-77,	216	121,448
1852,	164	83,015	1877-78,	278	131,363
1853,	184	88,434	1878-79,	239	122,370
1854,	125	49,293	1879-80, { Relief, 2,144; Ordinary, 463 }	2,607	a 331,510
1855,	98	65,160	1880-81,	638	a 784,659
1856,	108	33,910	1881-82,	401	a 235,563
1857,	114	81,674	1882-83,	491	a 138,536
1858,	119	35,394	1883-84,	303	a 123,063
1859,	111	73,346	1884-85,	333	a 117,190
1860,	139	64,903	1885-86,	396	ab 70,078
1861,	164	36,636	1886-87,	219	ab 59,103
1862,	184	61,378	1887-88,	181	b 44,753
1863,	128	48,830	1888-89,	148	b 31,743
1864,	132	66,130	1889-90,	179	b 33,077
1865,	90	18,216	1890-91,	213	b 29,764
1866,	98	76,293	1891-92,	207	b 34,806
1867,	163	33,180	1892-93,	221	30,871
1868-9,	179	64,973	1893-94,	223	32,391
1869-70,	168	83,578	1894-95,	313	33,080
1870-71,	169	77,980			
1871-72,	160	82,533			

(a) Including Relief of Distress Loans. (b) Including loans under 31st Section of the Land Law (Ireland) Act, 1881.

The business done under this service reached its lowest point in number of applications in 1888-89. Since that year there has been a decided increase. The number of applications received during the year 1894-95 was 342, showing an increase of nearly 5 per cent. on those received during the previous year. About one-third of the applicants are purchasers under the Land Purchase Acts, and it is probable that this class will avail itself largely of loans under the Land Improvement Acts.

Classification of loans under which works were *commenced* in 1894-95:—

Class of Work.	No. of Loans under which works were commenced.	Amount Sanctioned.	Average of each Loan.
		£	£
Drainage and other Land Works,	13	1,500	158
Farm Buildings,	180	21,365	119
Labourers' Cottages,	18	1,149	248
Mixed Loans—including Buildings and Land Works,	15	2,210	149
Totals,	225	29,964	—
General Average per Loan,	—	—	133

The following Table shows the certified expenditure on the various classes of works under loans *completed* during the year ending 31st March, 1895:—

	£	s.	d.
Field Works,	13,801	13	4
Farm Buildings,	35,447	10	6
Labourers' Cottages,	3,000	3	8
Scotch Mills,	—		
Planting for Shelter,	996	6	6
	£53,117	11	11

The following table gives the number of Land Improvement loans made, and the sums issued in the several counties of Ireland up to the 31st March, 1895 :—

SCHEDULE showing the NUMBER of LOANS and AMOUNTS issued from commencement of ACT.

Name of County.	No. of Loans.	Amount Issued.			Total No. of Loans.	Total Amount Issued.		
		£	s.	d.		£	s.	d.
NORTHERN DIVISION.								
Antrim, ...	311	153,833	0	0				
Londonderry, . . .	173	70,548	0	0				
Donegal, ...	380	183,034	0	0				
Fermanagh, . . .	167	81,708	0	0				
Tyrone, ...	[illegible]	147,883	0	0				
Armagh, ...	69	31,928	0	0				
Down, ...	169	94,874	0	0	1,411	746,479	0	0
MIDLAND AND EASTERN.								
Cavan, . . .	180	84,710	0	0				
Monaghan, . . .	105	44,004	0	0				
Longford, ...	330	181,768	0	0				
Louth, ...	116	42,736	0	0				
Meath, ...	613	202,860	0	0				
Westmeath, . . .	333	97,863	0	0				
Dublin, ...	305	81,114	0	0				
Kildare, ...	301	142,467	0	0				
King's, ...	236	61,369	0	0				
Queen's, ...	450	154,290	0	0				
Wicklow, ...	301	123,443	0	0				
Carlow, ...	735	107,319	0	0				
Kilkenny, ...	318	90,731	0	0				
Wexford, ...	328	131,880	0	0	3,653	1,511,513	0	0
WESTERN.								
Sligo, ...	293	128,447	0	0				
Leitrim, ...	198	74,770	0	0				
Mayo, ...	809	278,866	0	0				
Roscommon, . . .	671	228,303	0	0				
Galway, . . .	989	336,963	0	0				
Clare, ...	489	172,048	0	0	2,772	1,180,607	0	0
SOUTHERN.								
Limerick, ...	824	373,572	0	0				
Tipperary, . . .	644	311,830	0	0				
Waterford, . . .	321	76,016	0	0				
Cork, ...	1,367	422,297	0	0				

Main and Thorough Drainage or other Field Works.

The number of Land Improvement loans sanctioned for works, of which thorough drainage forms the principal part, since the commencement in 1847 to the 31st March in this year, is 8,226, for £3,716,797, and of this number 20, for £4,280, were approved during the year ended 31st March, 1895.

Planting for Shelter.

Since the passing of the Act 29 and 30 Vic., c. 40, under which advances are made for this purpose, 125 loans, amounting to £28,050, have been made, and of that number 3, for £765, were sanctioned during the year.

Farm Buildings.

Under this head 3,196 loans have been sanctioned since the passing of the Act 13 and 14 Vic., c. 19, the amount being £1,312,360. This includes 205 loans, for £26,745, approved during the past financial year.

Dwellings for Agricultural Labourers.

For this class of work the number of loans sanctioned since the passing of the Act 23 Vic., c. 19, which first authorised such advances, is 768, for £350,654, 22 of which, amounting to £4,794, were approved in the year.

Under section 19 of the Land Law (Ireland) Act, 1881, we have power to make advances to tenant farmers, who, pursuant to the injunctions of the Irish Land Commission, and as a condition attached to the fixing of a "fair rent," proceed to erect labourers' dwellings on their holdings. Such tenants are deemed to be persons to whom a loan may be made under the Landed Property Improvement (Ireland) Acts, for the improvement or building of dwellings for labourers, as if such persons were owners within the meaning of the Act 10 Vic., c. 32, sec. 7. One loan for £21 was sanctioned under this section within the year ending 31st March, 1895. Under this provision 258 loans, amounting to £15,990, have been sanctioned since the Act came into operation, the instalments issued amounting to £13,664.

Advances for this purpose are also made under section 31 of the Land Law Act, 1881. See Table of Expenditure under this section, p. 37.

The following Table shows the number and amount of Loans sanctioned for Dwellings for Agricultural Labourers under the Act 23 Vic., cap. 19, and the Land Law (Ireland) Act, 1881, sec. 19, since the passing of the Labourers' Acts, 1883 and 1885.

Year.	23 Vic., c. 19.		Land Law (Ireland) Act, 1881, sec. 19.	
	No. of Loans Sanctioned.	Amount Sanctioned.	No. of Loans Sanctioned.	Amount Issued.
		£		£
1883,	37	13,210	26	833
1884,	36	15,496	41	1,818
1885,	33	8,913	64	5,039
1886,	35	7,535	37	3,698
1887,	18	6,700	11	1,468
1888,	19	6,365	24	419
1889,	13	4,090	3	146
1890,	11	3,005	1	286
1891,	17	4,885	6	221
1892,	10	1,940	2	169
1893,	20	4,005	Nil.	116
1894,	14	4,385	Nil.	29
1895,	21	4,770	1	4

Loans to Tenants for Improvement of Holdings, or "Land Law Loans."

(See p. 16).

Land Law (Ireland) Act, 1881, Section 31.

Under section 31 of the above Act, under which loans to tenants are generally made, the number of loans sanctioned since our last report was 479, amounting to £40,125, the sum issued being £36,360. This makes the total of loans sanctioned under the section from the date of the Act to 31st March, 1895, 12,205—amount sanctioned, £1,049,232, the instalments issued reaching £990,697.

The number of applications for loans lodged during the year 1894–95 was 778, being an increase of 28 from last year. Of this number 40 were received from occupying owners, who were prevented by some feature in their application from proceeding under the Land Improvement Act.

The following table gives the distribution by Counties of the sums issued for all classes of work under the 31st Section of the Land Law (Ireland) Act, 1881 :—

SCHEDULE showing the NUMBER of LOANS SANCTIONED and AMOUNTS ISSUED up to the 31st MARCH, 1895.

PROVINCE AND COUNTY	Number of Loans Sanctioned.			Amounts Sanctioned.			Total Issues.		
	To 31st Mar., 1894.	Year ending 31st Mar., 1895.	Total Sanctioned.	To 31st Mar., 1894.	Year ending 31st Mar., 1895.	Total Sanctioned.	To 31st Mar., 1894.	Year ending 31st Mar., 1895.	Total Issues.
LEINSTER:				£	£	£	£	£	£
Carlow, . .	74	9	83	9,453	1,840	11,293	6,888	115	7,003
Dublin, . .	121	17	138	18,616	1,354	20,070	15,457	2,973	17,487
Kildare, . .	148	13	161	23,469	1,460	24,929	18,129	1,062	20,191
Kilkenny, . .	134	33	168	16,725	1,565	18,290	11,018	1,442	12,460
King's, . .	210	13	223	19,915	1,200	21,115	16,768	440	17,208
Longford, . .	297	7	304	26,505	485	26,990	22,443	780	23,313
Louth, . .	53	11	64	7,535	1,105	8,640	6,463	850	7,313
Meath, . .	182	18	200	30,080	2,350	32,030	24,649	2,470	27,119
Queen's, . .	116	11	127	11,083	1,000	12,083	8,423	953	9,376
Westmeath, . .	261	15	276	25,730	1,010	26,740	23,036	2,051	25,137
Wexford, . .	143	11	154	13,640	1,080	14,720	11,874	869	12,743
Wicklow, . .	123	3	126	13,430	370	13,800	11,610	264	11,876
Totals,	1,876	148	2,031	216,273	14,920	231,200	177,312	13,022	190,334
MUNSTER:									
Clare, . .	664	10	674	36,190	630	36,780	18,487	629	19,116
Cork, . .	2,016	95	2,111	173,473	8,090	181,563	129,673	7,830	137,503
Kerry, . .	874	48	922	67,333	3,730	71,063	53,838	3,165	57,003
Limerick, . .	653	44	697	61,425	3,630	65,055	51,033	2,287	53,320
Tipperary, . .	583	33	616	34,700	3,446	38,146	45,176	4,624	50,210
Waterford, . .	80	10	90	4,350	618	5,000	6,033	1,044	7,067
Totals,	4,865	259	5,124	421,473	20,250	441,723	353,636	18,015	371,551
ULSTER:									
Antrim, . .	111	9	120	11,603	436	12,039	10,143	345	10,181
Armagh, . .	81	4	85	5,913	250	6,165	4,783	43	4,817
Cavan, . .	634	6	640	40,735	285	41,020	37,088	253	37,143
Donegal, . .	266	1	267	18,377	70	18,447	17,380	77	17,457
Down, . .	73	3	76	7,159	436	7,855	6,671	326	6,997
Fermanagh, . .	164	4	168	10,951	348	11,260	8,899	169	9,068
Londonderry, . .	128	0	128	10,163	—	10,163	9,103	119	9,222
Monaghan, . .	80	4	84	7,200	320	7,521	4,943	600	5,543
Tyrone, . .	247	3	250	18,420	178	18,598	15,847	146	15,993
Totals,	1,803	36	1,838	138,852	2,350	139,202	116,268	1,876	118,144
CONNAUGHT:									
Galway, . .	602	13	614	48,330	730	49,030	42,051	684	42,735
Leitrim, . .	606	4	610	38,170	715	38,885	34,146	253	34,194
Mayo, . .	953	3	956	71,300	270	71,570	62,147	297	62,444
Roscommon, . .	820	11	831	60,240	705	60,945	34,017	761	34,778
Sligo, . .	670	8	678	32,415	675	34,080	32,625	477	33,102
Totals,	3,163	38	3,201	235,874	2,856	237,918	206,189	2,454	206,643
Grand Totals,	11,716	479	12,180	1,008,107	40,125	1,048,232	854,837	38,340	890,097

We also beg to submit a statement classifying the loans in which works have been completed under the different descriptions of work, to the 31st March, 1895:—

Description of Work.	Amount Expended		
	From passing of Act to 31st March, 1894.	For year ending 31st March, 1895.	Total from passing of Act to 31st March, 1895.
	£ s. d.	£ s. d.	£ s. d.
Drainage, Fencing, Farm Roads, and other Land Works,	404,168 0 1	8,1[illegible] 19 3	412,804 19 4
Farm Houses and Offices,	480,838 17 7	28,369 11 10	469,108 9 5
Labourers' Cottages, 18th section,	10,162 13 10	Nil.	10,152 13 10
Labourers' Cottages, 31st section,	13,762 1 6	459 0 9	14,221 2 3
Scutch Mills for Flax,	936 13 6	Nil.	936 13 6
	860,155 6 6	47,227 11 10	907,383 18 4

The number of loans in which the amounts sanctioned have been expended and the works certified as completed, is 10,293, and those in which the works were still in progress on the 31st March, 1895, were 406.

CLASS (4).—MISCELLANEOUS LOANS.

Glebe Loans. No. 30 in *Abstract*, p. 42.

Forty-nine applications for loans have been received during the year, amounting to £13,476, and 36 loans, for £10,813, have been granted. The issues for the year have amounted to £9,450. Since the passing of the first Act, in 1870, we have received 1,481 applications, of which the following is an abstract of those on which issues were made to 31st March, 1895:—

—	No.	Amount.
		£
Church of Ireland,	783	153,[illegible]
Roman Catholic,	648	297,078
Presbyterian,	309	68,526
Wesleyan and other,	69	23,183
	1,259	530,77[illegible]

Loans for National School Teachers' Residences. No. 35 in *Abstract*, p. 42.

Forty-eight applications for loans have been received during the year, amounting to £11,180, and 37 loans have been sanctioned for £8,805. The total advances for loans of this kind up to 31st March, 1895, was £155,417 10s. 0d. The number and amount of loans sanctioned continue to decline as compared with the year 1891-2, in spite of the existence of the powers given by the National Education (Ireland) Act, 1892, for the compulsory acquisition of sites.

Loans for Building Schools and Training Colleges. No. 36 in *Abstract*, p. 42.

Eighteen applications for loans have been received during the year, amounting to £4,160, and eighteen loans, amounting to £3,429, have been sanctioned.

IRISH CHURCH FUND LOANS.

No loans or advances under previous loans were made from this fund during the year.

Out of £1,289,932 advanced from the Irish Church Fund under the Relief of Distress Act of 1880, £550,204 has been repaid, £29,296 has been remitted, and of the balance outstanding, £690,432, £681,495 is not yet due, and £8,937 is in arrear. The arrears have decreased during the year by £315.

The rate of interest on these loans is 1 per cent., but borrowers paying land improvement and arterial drainage charges, are allowed to redeem their principal liabilities on the basis of 3 per cent. interest. The principal cancelled by such redemptions now amounts to £10,227, including £960 in the present year.

RATES OF INTEREST.

The following statement shows the rates of interest chargeable on the several amounts making the aggregate balances in each year ended 31st March, 1893, 1894, and 1895 respectively:—

—	31 March, 1893.	31 March, 1894.	31 March, 1895.
	£	£	£
Free of Interest,	15,489	13,473	12,753
2 per cent.,	6,000	6,000	6,000
2¾ "	1,016,524	1,105,935	1,113,713
3 "	565,373	566,770	616,735
3¼ "	147,836	158,719	181,534
3½ "	2,702,710	2,812,918	2,950,594
3¾ "	758,851	760,325	737,984
4 "	1,504,164	1,465,193	1,374,601
4½ "	234,020	234,191	272,450
5 "	46,908	49,505	47,257
Advances on which interest is deferred, pending the completion of the works,	88,006	96,896	104,154
Total Local Loans Fund,	7,716,697	7,760,577	7,750,134
Church Fund Loans— at 3 per cent.,	790,135	720,013	690,131
	*8,506,832	†8,480,590	‡8,259,648

* Exclusive of £214,930 written off from the Account of the Assets of the Local Loans Fund.
† " £197,102 " " "
‡ " £197,016 " " "

The average rate chargeable on the advances out of the Local Loans Fund was £3 11s. 0d. on the 31st March, 1893; £3 11s. 2d. on the 31st March, 1894; and £3 11s. 0d. on the 31st March, 1895. The interest realised in the year averaged £3 5s. 2d. per cent. on the principal sum outstanding on the 1st April, 1894.

The following is an Abstract of Loans made by the Commissioners of Public Works, showing the Amounts Remitted, and

No.	Acts under which Advances have been made.	Purposes for which Advanced.	No. of Loans up to 31st March, 1895.	Advanced or Remitted: In the Year ended 31st March, 1895.	Advanced or Remitted: Total up to the 31st March, 1895.	Principal: In the Year ending: Paid.
		I. Public Works Loans, 1 & 2 Wm. IV., c. 33, and 40 & 41 Vic., c. 27.				
		Class I.—Loans secured on Undertakings.		£ s. d.	£ s. d.	£ s. d.
1	1 & 2 Wm. IV., c. 33,	Land Drainage—various works,	[illegible]	—	484,834 0 0	33,709 [illegible]
2	Do.	Inland Navigation,	6	—	152,209 4 5	[illegible]
3	Do.	Railways,	27	8,000 0 0	1,159,128 10 11	118,813 [illegible]
4	Do.	Quarries, Mines, &c.,	8	800 0 0	95,011 19 0	164 11 [illegible]
5	Do.	Harbours, Docks, &c.,	[illegible]	71,850 0 0	544,433 1 7	1,403 9 11
6	Do.	Reclamation of Waste Lands,	—	—	138,891 0 0	—
7	39 & 40 Vic., c. 44,	Labourers' Dwellings in Towns,	41	—	149,911 15 0	4,371 [illegible]
8	53 & 54 Vic., c. 70,	Housing of the Working Classes,	113	34,885 14 0	380,388 0 9	14,094 [illegible]
			[illegible]	[illegible]	3,714,[illegible]	172,494 [illegible]
		Class II.—Loans secured on Rates.				
9	1 & 2 Wm. IV., c. 33,	Grand Juries of Counties for Roads, Court Houses, &c.,	[illegible]	[illegible]	788,[illegible]	7,[illegible]
10	Do.	Roads and Bridges,	7	—	[illegible]	[illegible]
11	40 & 41 Vic., c. 11 & 54; 44 & 45 Vic., c. [illegible]; 46 Vic., c. 45,	Public Buildings; Public Libraries; Reformatories, and Industrial Schools,	11	1,[illegible] 0 0	[illegible]	[illegible]
12	9 Vic., c. 3,	Fishery Piers and Harbours,	1	—	33,344 17 3	[illegible]
13	57 Geo. III., c. 34,	Public Works Loans,	1	—	[illegible]	—
14	1 & 2 Wm. IV., c. [illegible],	Repairs of Post Roads and Bridges,	9	334 3 1	184,[illegible]	434 14 4
15	10 & 11 Vic., c. [illegible],	Repairs of Fishery Piers and Harbours,	4	1,640 6 0	18,[illegible]	—
16	31 & 32 Vic., c. [illegible],	Maintenance of Navigation Works,	1	—	[illegible]	[illegible]
17	1 & 2 Geo. IV., c. 33; 18 & 19 Vic., c. 109,	Lunatic Asylums Buildings,	[illegible]	79,[illegible]	1,4[illegible]	[illegible]
18	38 & 39 Vic., c. [illegible],	Artisans' Dwellings,	5	—	61,[illegible]	[illegible]
19	37 & 38 Vic., c. [illegible]; 41 & 42 Vic., c. 52,	Public Health,	[illegible]	130,[illegible]	2,017,[illegible]	[illegible]
20	45 & 46 Vic., c. 47,	Emigration,	[illegible]	—	11,[illegible]	[illegible]
21	46 & 47 Vic., c. 60,	Labourers Acts,	2,[illegible]	[illegible]	1,[illegible]	[illegible]
22	45 & 46 Vic., c. [illegible],	Dispensary Houses,	[illegible]	[illegible]	[illegible]	[illegible]
			[illegible]	[illegible]	7,1[illegible]	[illegible]
		Class III.—Loans secured on Lands.				
23	5 & 6 Vic., c. 89,	Arterial Drainage and Navigation,	5	—	2,[illegible]	[illegible]
24	26 & 27 Vic., c. 88,	River Drainage,	1,[illegible]	[illegible]	[illegible]	[illegible]
25	29 & 30 Vic., c. [illegible],	River Drainage Maintenance,	[illegible]	[illegible]	44,[illegible]	[illegible]

(Continued on next page.)

Advances and Repayments in the Year, the Total Advances and Repayments to the 31st March, 1895, the the Balances Outstanding.

[Repaid] and REPAYMENT paid by Borrowers.				BALANCES Outstanding against Borrowers on 31st March, 1895.				
[to] 31st March, 1895.	Total to 31st of March, 1895.		Remitted.	Principal			Interest.	No.
				In Arrear.		Not yet due.		
Interest.	Principal.	Interest.		Written off from the Accounts of Arrears of the Local Loans Fund.	Other Arrears.			
£ s. d.	£ s. d.	£ s. d.	£ s. d.	£ s. d.	£ s. d.	£ s. d.	£ s. d.	
[illegible]	[illegible]	[illegible]	—	—	[illegible]	[illegible]	[illegible]	1
[illegible]	[illegible]	[illegible]	[illegible]	[illegible]	[illegible]	[illegible]	[illegible]	2
[illegible]	[illegible]	[illegible]	—	[illegible]	[illegible]	[illegible]	[illegible]	3
[illegible]	[illegible]	[illegible]	—	—	—	[illegible]	—	4
[illegible]	[illegible]	[illegible]	[illegible]	—	[illegible]	[illegible]	[illegible]	5
—	[illegible]	[illegible]	—	[illegible]	—	—	—	6
[illegible]	[illegible]	[illegible]	[illegible]	[illegible]	[illegible]	[illegible]	[illegible]	7
[illegible]	[illegible]	[illegible]	—	—	[illegible]	[illegible]	[illegible]	8
[illegible]	[illegible]	[illegible]	[illegible]	[illegible]	[illegible]	[illegible]	[illegible]	
[illegible]	[illegible]	[illegible]	—	—	—	[illegible]	—	9
[illegible]	[illegible]	[illegible]	[illegible]	—	—	[illegible]	—	10
[illegible]	[illegible]	[illegible]	[illegible]	—	[illegible]	[illegible]	—	11
[illegible]	[illegible]	[illegible]	—	—	—	[illegible]	—	12
[illegible]	[illegible]	[illegible]	[illegible]	—	—	[illegible]	—	13
[illegible]	[illegible]	[illegible]	—	—	—	[illegible]	—	14
—	[illegible]	[illegible]	[illegible]	—	—	[illegible]	—	15
[illegible]	[illegible]	[illegible]	—	—	—	—	—	16
[illegible]	[illegible]	[illegible]	[illegible]	—	—	[illegible]	—	17
[illegible]	[illegible]	[illegible]	—	—	—	[illegible]	—	18
[illegible]	[illegible]	[illegible]	—	—	[illegible]	[illegible]	[illegible]	19
[illegible]	[illegible]	[illegible]	—	—	[illegible]	[illegible]	[illegible]	20

The following is an Abstract of Loans made by the Commissioners of Public Works, showing the Amounts remitted, and

No.	Acts under which Advanced [illegible]	PURPOSES FOR WHICH ADVANCED.	No. of [illegible] Loans [illegible] 1895.	Advanced in Ireland: In the Year ended 31st March, 1895.	Advanced in Ireland: Total up to the 31st March, 1895.	Principal: In the Year ended: Principal.
		CLASS III.—continued.		£ s. d.	£ s. d.	£ s. d.
[illegible]	[illegible] Vic., c. [illegible], sec. 1; [illegible] & [illegible] Vic., c. [illegible], sec. [illegible]	Improvement of Lands—viz., Drainage, Erection of Farm Buildings and Farm Labourers' Dwellings, Planting for Shelter,	[illegible]	[illegible] 0 0	4,1[illegible] 1 10	[illegible] 0 2
[illegible]	[illegible] Vic., c. [illegible], s. [illegible],	Land Improvement Preliminary Expenses,	1	1,[illegible] 0 0	[illegible] 0 0	[illegible] 0 2
[illegible]	[illegible] & [illegible] Vic., c. [illegible], s. [illegible].	Land Law.—Advances to Occupiers of Land for Improvement of their Holdings,	[illegible]	[illegible] 0 0	[illegible] 0 0	[illegible] 5
[illegible]	[illegible] & [illegible] Vic., c. [illegible],	For Advances to Tenants for Purchase of their Farms, &c.,	[illegible]	—	[illegible] [illegible] 7	[illegible] 11 1
			[illegible]	[illegible] 11 1	[illegible] 0 0	[illegible] [illegible] 1
		CLASS IV.—Miscellaneous Loans.				
[illegible]	[illegible] & [illegible] Vic., c. [illegible], &c.	Glebe Loans,	1,[illegible]	[illegible] 18 0	[illegible] [illegible] 0	[illegible] [illegible]
[illegible]	[illegible] Geo. III., c. [illegible]; [illegible] Geo. IV., c. [illegible].	Building Schools,	[illegible]	—	[illegible] 0 7	[illegible] 0
[illegible]	[illegible] Vic., c. 1,	Seed Supply,	[illegible]	—	[illegible] 11 10	..
[illegible]	[illegible] Vic., c. 1,	Do.,	[illegible]	—	[illegible] 14 1	[illegible] 3
[illegible]	[illegible] Vic., c. [illegible]	Do.,	[illegible]	[illegible] [illegible]	[illegible] [illegible]	—
[illegible]	[illegible] & [illegible] Vic., c. [illegible],	National School Teachers' Residences,	[illegible]	[illegible] 0 0	[illegible] 10 0	[illegible] 0
[illegible]	[illegible] & [illegible] Vic., c. [illegible],	Non-Vested Schools and Training Colleges,	[illegible]	[illegible] 0 0	[illegible] [illegible]	[illegible]
			[illegible]	[illegible] 0 0	[illegible] [illegible] 10	[illegible] 1
		Total Current and Unclosed Services,	[illegible]	[illegible] 0 7	[illegible] 17 11	[illegible] 17 1
		Add Total Closed Services,	—	—	[illegible] 6 10	—
		Gross Total Local Loans Fund,	[illegible]	[illegible] 0 1	[illegible]	[illegible] 11 7
		II. Irish Church Fund Loans.				
		CLASS II.—Loans secured on Rates.				
[illegible]	[illegible] Vic., c. [illegible]; [illegible] & [illegible] Vic., c. [illegible].	Public Health,	[illegible]	—	[illegible] 10 0	[illegible]
[illegible]	Do.,	Seaboard Works,	[illegible]	—	[illegible] [illegible]	[illegible]
[illegible]	Do.,	Relief of Distress,	[illegible]	—	11,[illegible] [illegible] 4	[illegible]
[illegible]	Do.,	Relief of Distress Grants,	—	—	[illegible] 0 0	..
			[illegible]	—	[illegible] 17 3	[illegible]
		CLASS III.—Loans secured on Lands.				
[illegible]	Do.,	Improvement of Lands,	[illegible]	—	[illegible] 17 6	[illegible]
[illegible]	Do.,	Arterial Drainage,	[illegible]	—	[illegible] 1 0	[illegible]
			[illegible]	—	[illegible] 18 [illegible]	[illegible]
		Total Irish Church Fund Loans,	[illegible]	—	[illegible] 10 1	[illegible] 1
		Grand Total,	[illegible]	[illegible] 0 7	[illegible] 0 [illegible]	[illegible]

Advances and Repayments in the Year, the Total Advances and Repayments to the 31st March, 1895, the the Balances Outstanding—continued.

[illegible]	[illegible]		[illegible]	[illegible]					
[illegible]	[illegible]			[illegible]					
Interest.	Principal.	Interest.	Remitted.	[illegible]	[illegible]	[illegible]	[illegible]	Interest.	No.
£ s. d.	£ s. d.	£ s. d.	£ s. d.	£ s. d.	£ s. d.	£ s. d.	£ s. d.		
[illegible]	[illegible]	[illegible]	—	[illegible]	[illegible]	[illegible]	[illegible]	26
..	[illegible]	—	[illegible]	[illegible]	—	[illegible]	—	27
[illegible]	[illegible]	[illegible]	—	[illegible]	[illegible]	[illegible]	[illegible]	28
[illegible]	[illegible]	[illegible]	—	—	[illegible]	[illegible]	[illegible]	29
[illegible]	[illegible]	[illegible]	[illegible]	[illegible]	[illegible]	[illegible]	[illegible]	
[illegible]	[illegible]	[illegible]	—	—	[illegible]	[illegible]	[illegible]	30
[illegible]	[illegible]	[illegible]	[illegible]	—	—	[illegible]	--	31
—	[illegible]	[illegible]	—	—	[illegible]	—	—	32
[illegible]	[illegible]	[illegible]	—	—	[illegible]	—	—	33
—	—	—	—	—	—	[illegible]	—	34
[illegible]	[illegible]	[illegible]	—	—	[illegible]	[illegible]	[illegible]	35
[illegible]	[illegible]	[illegible]	—	—	—	[illegible]	..	36
[illegible]	[illegible]	[illegible]	[illegible]	—	[illegible]	[illegible]	[illegible]	
[illegible]	[illegible]	[illegible]	[illegible]	—	—	—	—	
—	[illegible]	[illegible]	[illegible]	—	—	—	—	
[illegible]	[illegible]	[illegible]	[illegible]	[illegible]	[illegible]	[illegible]	[illegible]	
					[illegible]			
[illegible]	[illegible]	[illegible]	—	—	[illegible]	[illegible]	[illegible]	37
[illegible]	[illegible]	[illegible]	[illegible]	—	—	[illegible]	—	38
[illegible]	[illegible]	[illegible]		—	[illegible]	—	[illegible]	39
—	—	—	[illegible]	—	—	—	—	40
[illegible]	[illegible]	[illegible]	[illegible]	—	[illegible]	[illegible]	[illegible]	
[illegible]	[illegible]	[illegible]	[illegible]	—	[illegible]	[illegible]	[illegible]	41
[illegible]	[illegible]	[illegible]	—	—	7 14 10	[illegible]	[illegible]	42
[illegible]	[illegible]	[illegible]	[illegible]	—	[illegible]	[illegible]	[illegible]	
[illegible]	[illegible]	[illegible]	[illegible]	—	[illegible]	[illegible]	[illegible]	
[illegible]	[illegible]	[illegible]	[illegible]		[illegible] [illegible]		[illegible] (c)	

* [illegible]

† [illegible]

‡ [illegible]

(c) [illegible]

APPENDIX D.—

(D.)—Abstract of the Accounts of the Commissioners of Public Works in Ireland, showing the Total of

Reference to Appendix	Page	Heads of Account	Balances on 31st March, 1894	Receipts
			£ s. d.	£ s. d.
D 1	44–51	Parliamentary Votes and Grants, viz.:— 1. Public Works and Buildings, Ireland; 2. Railways, Ireland; 3. Tralee and Dingle Light Railway; 4. Public Works Office, Ireland; 5. Suspense Account; 6. Relief of Distress; 7. Appropriations in Aid, Public Works and Buildings	12,[illegible] 8 4	416,[illegible] 4 6
D 2	51–53	Loans Advanced,	33,767 3 10	4[illegible],0[illegible] 9 0
D 3	54–55	Loans Repayments,	—	3[illegible],[illegible]4 9 6
D 4	55–56	Land Improvement Preliminaries, 19 Vic. c. [illegible],	209 19 4	2,[illegible]7 1 1
D 5	56–57	District Lunatic Asylums,	2,128 13 4	109,310 6 1
D 6	58–59	Sea Fisheries, Ireland, 46 & 47 Vic., c. 26,	4,1[illegible] 17 6	2,[illegible] 12 9
D 7	60–63	Miscellaneous Services, viz.:— (items 1–14)	2,[illegible] 19 6	45,1[illegible] 16 3
		Total,	48,016 15 7	1,[illegible] 2 6
D 8	64–65	Statement of Final Awards under Arterial Drainage Act, 26 & 27 Vic., c. 88, with Repayments thereon, to the 31st March, 1895.		

Miscellaneous Services (D 7), viz.:—

1. Deposit Accounts, 1 & 2 Wm. IV., c. 33, &c.,
2. Railway and other Arbitrations, 14 & 15 Vic., c. 70,
3. Arterial Drainage Deposits, 26 & 27 Vic., c. 88, &c.,
4. Piers—Works, 1 & 2 Wm. IV., c. 33, &c.,
5. Piers—Repairs, 16 & 17 Vic., c. 136,
6. Inland Navigations—Shannon,
7. Drainage Maintenance, 29 & 30 Vic., c. 49,
8. National Monuments, 38 & 39 Vic., c. 41,
9. Sea and Coast Fisheries Loan Fund, 47 & 48 Vic., c. 21, &c.,
10. Linen Hall,
11. Galway Harbour Receiver's Account,
12. Southern Railway,
13. Letterkenny Railway,
14. Sundry Accounts,

Office of Public Works, Dublin, 18th May, 1895.

Accounts.

Sums intrusted to their Management for Collection or Disbursement for Year ended 31st March, 1895

[illegible]	[illegible]	[illegible]	Paid.	[illegible]	[illegible]
£ s. d.	£ s. d.	£ s. d.	£ s. d.	£ s. d.	£ s. d.
—	437,[illegible] 16 1	—	431,[illegible] 5 6	6,[illegible] 1 5	437,[illegible] 16 1
—	503,747 8 10	—	477,718 8 7	26,[illegible] 1 5	503,747 8 10
—	783,374 8 6	—	783,374 8 6	—	783,374 8 6
—	2,[illegible] 0 5	—	2,049 0 7	138 18 11	2,[illegible] 0 5
—	112,455 19 4	—	104,481 0 1	7,914 10 3	111,450 18 5
—	7,[illegible] 1 8	—	[illegible] 9 1	6,[illegible] 3 6	7,[illegible] 4 5
—	41,486 15 8	—	25,[illegible] 14 11	16,[illegible] 0 10	41,486 15 9
—	1,[illegible] 1 8	—	1,[illegible],[illegible] 11 2	63,187 16 1	1,[illegible],920 1 5

G. H. [illegible], Accountant.

An Account showing the Receipts and Expenditure of the Commissioners

(D 1.)—PARLIAMENTARY

RECEIPTS.	£ s. d.	£ s. d.	£ s. d.
Balance from last Account,	—	—	12,421 8 8
Public Works and Buildings.			
Vote for the year 1894–95,	—	103,119 6 0	
New Works and Alterations:—			
Transfers and Re-lodgements,	—	219 4 1	

of Public Works in the Year ended 31st March, 1895.

VOTES AND GRANTS.

EXPENDITURE.		£ s. d.	£ s. d.	£ s. d.
Balances on Parliamentary Votes surrendered to H.M. Exchequer, viz.:—				
Public Works and Buildings,		—	1,648 2 2	
Office of Public Works,		—	712 1 2	
Railways, Ireland,		—	460 16 11	
				2,710 9 3
Public Works and Buildings:—				
Purchase of Sites and Buildings,		—	457 6 0	
New Works and Alterations:—				
Royal Hospital,		63 2 1		
Royal Hibernian Military School,		1,097 0 11		
Coastguard Buildings,		7,165 7 9		
Naval Reserve Buildings,		2,059 10 3		
Ordnance Survey Buildings,		1,114 10 2		
State Residences,		131 3 4		
Chief Secretary's Office,		493 14 10		
Stationery Office,		26 7 6		
Registrar General's Office,		3,387 1 2		
General Survey and Valuation Office,		87 13 8		
High Court of Justice,		115 3 10		
Registry of Deeds,		118 8 5		
Registry of Titles,		39 8 6		
Probate Offices,		41 15 0		
Land Commission Court and Offices,		1,133 18 9		
Metropolitan Police Buildings,		608 2 10		
Constabulary,		3,164 8 10		
Dundrum Criminal Lunatic Asylum,		3,636 15 3		
Science and Art Buildings,		2,128 8 6		
National Education Buildings:—				
Munster Model Farm,	£351 11 3			
Ordinary Literary Schools,	£26,170 5 3			
Waterford Model School,	£71 7 3			
Metropolitan Buildings,	£28 5 3			
		26,621 8 10		
Green-street Court House,		1,000 0 0		
Queen's Colleges,		710 10 3		
Inland Revenue,		96 11 3		
Postal and Telegraph Buildings,		6,157 5 3		
Phoenix Park,		449 12 4		
Kingstown Harbour,		10,046 0 0		
Arterial Drainage—Bann District,		2,000 0 0		
Arklow Harbour,		1,750 0 0		
Boyne Navigation,		703 11 7		
			82,609 10 6	
Carried forward,		—	83,066 16 6	2,710 2 3

An Account showing the Receipts and Expenditure of the Commissioners

(D 1.)—PARLIAMENTARY

RECEIPTS—*continued.*

	£ s. d.	£ s. d.	£ s. d.
Brought forward,		169,358 4 1	15,4[illegible]
1. Public Works and Buildings—*continued.*			
Transfers and Extrapayments:—			
Maintenance and Supplies,	674 1 2		
Furniture, Fittings, &c.,	103 6 6		
Fuel, Light, Water, &c.,	25 1 4		
Drainage Works—River Shannon,	6 4 6		
		808 13 6	
			170,166 17 7

of Public Works in the Year ended 31st March, 1895—continued.

VOTES AND GRANTS—continued.

EXPENDITURE—continued.

	Maintenance and Supplies. £ s. d.	Furniture, Fittings, and Utensils. £ s. d.	Rent and Insurance. £ s. d.	Fuel, Light, Water, Cleaning, &c. £ s. d.	Totals. £ s. d.	£ s. d.	£ s. d.
Brought forward,	—	—	—	—	—	[illegible] 16 6	[illegible] 2 3
Public Works and Buildings—con.							
Royal Hospital, Kilmainham,	[illegible]	[illegible]	—	[illegible]	[illegible]		
Royal Hibernian Military School,	[illegible]	[illegible]	—	[illegible]	[illegible]		
[illegible] Buildings,	[illegible]	[illegible]	—	—	[illegible]		
[illegible] Buildings,	[illegible]	[illegible]	—	—	[illegible]		
Ord. Survey, Mountjoy Barracks,	[illegible]	[illegible]	[illegible]	[illegible]	[illegible]		
Dublin Castle, State Apartments and Chapel Royal,	[illegible]	[illegible]	[illegible]	[illegible]	[illegible]		
[illegible] House in Castle,	[illegible]	[illegible]	—	—	[illegible]		
Viceregal Lodge, Gardens, &c.,	[illegible]	[illegible]	—	[illegible]	[illegible]		
Private Secretary's Lodge,	[illegible]	[illegible]	—	[illegible]	[illegible]		
Chief Sec.'s Lodge, Gardens, &c.,	[illegible]	[illegible]	—	[illegible]	[illegible]		
Under Sec.'s Lodge and Demesne,	[illegible]	[illegible]	—	[illegible]	[illegible]		
Chief Sec.'s Office and Branches,	[illegible]	[illegible]	[illegible]	[illegible]	[illegible]		
[illegible] Offices,	[illegible]	[illegible]	—	[illegible]	[illegible]		
Civil Service Commissioners,	[illegible]	[illegible]	[illegible]	[illegible]	[illegible]		
Paymaster-General's Office,	[illegible]	[illegible]	—	[illegible]	[illegible]		
[illegible] Pension Office,	[illegible]	[illegible]	—	[illegible]	[illegible]		
Stationery Office,	[illegible]	[illegible]	[illegible]	[illegible]	[illegible]		
Quit Rent Office, [illegible]	[illegible]	[illegible]	[illegible]	[illegible]	[illegible]		
[illegible] Offices,	[illegible]	[illegible]	[illegible]	[illegible]	[illegible]		
Charitable Bequests Office,	[illegible]	[illegible]	[illegible]	[illegible]	[illegible]		
Local Government Board,	[illegible]	[illegible]	—	[illegible]	[illegible]		
Office of Public Works,	[illegible]	[illegible]	[illegible]	[illegible]	[illegible]		
Record Room and Offices,	[illegible]	[illegible]	—	[illegible]	[illegible]		
Registrar-General's and Census Office,	[illegible]	[illegible]	[illegible]	[illegible]	[illegible]		
[illegible] & Valuation Office,	[illegible]	[illegible]	[illegible]	[illegible]	[illegible]		
[illegible]	[illegible]	[illegible]	[illegible]	[illegible]	[illegible]		
High Court of Justice, Four Courts,	[illegible]	[illegible]	—	[illegible]	[illegible]		
[illegible] Court,	[illegible]	[illegible]	—	[illegible]	[illegible]		
Registry of Deeds, King's Inns,	[illegible]	[illegible]	—	[illegible]	[illegible]		
Record of Titles and Land Registration,	[illegible]	[illegible]	—	[illegible]	[illegible]		
[illegible] Offices,	[illegible]	[illegible]	[illegible]	[illegible]	[illegible]		
Registry of Judgments,	—	[illegible]	—	[illegible]	[illegible]		
Land Com. Court and Offices,	[illegible]	[illegible]	[illegible]	[illegible]	[illegible]		
[illegible], Police Courts and Offices in Dublin Castle,	[illegible]	[illegible]	[illegible]	[illegible]	[illegible]		
Metropolitan Police Stations,	[illegible]	[illegible]	[illegible]	[illegible]	[illegible]		
[illegible] Commissioners' Offices,	[illegible]	[illegible]	[illegible]	[illegible]	[illegible]		
Royal Irish Con. Depot & Offices in Dublin Castle,	[illegible]	[illegible]	—	[illegible]	[illegible]		
[illegible] Ireland,	[illegible]	[illegible]	—	—	[illegible]		
[illegible]	[illegible]	[illegible]	—	—	[illegible]		
[illegible] Offices,	[illegible]	[illegible]	—	[illegible]	[illegible]		
Reformatory and Industrial Schools Office,	[illegible]	[illegible]	—	[illegible]	[illegible]		
Dundrum Crim. Lunatic Asylum,	[illegible]	[illegible]	[illegible]	[illegible]	[illegible]		
Science and Art, Museum, Library, &c.,	[illegible]	[illegible]	[illegible]	[illegible]	[illegible]		
Botanic Gardens, Glasnevin,	[illegible]	[illegible]	[illegible]	[illegible]	[illegible]		
Royal College of Science,	[illegible]	[illegible]	[illegible]	[illegible]	[illegible]		
Geological Survey Office,	[illegible]	[illegible]	[illegible]	[illegible]	[illegible]		
[illegible] Offices and Schools of Nat. Educ. Department,	[illegible]	[illegible]	—	[illegible]	[illegible]		
Agricultural Model Schools, including Albert Model Farm,	[illegible]	[illegible]	—	[illegible]	[illegible]		
District and Minor Model Schools,	[illegible]	[illegible]	—	[illegible]	[illegible]		
National Schools,	[illegible]	[illegible]	—	—	[illegible]		
[illegible] Residences,	[illegible]	[illegible]	—	—	[illegible]		
National Gallery of Ireland,	[illegible]	[illegible]	—	[illegible]	[illegible]		
Queen's College, Cork,	[illegible]	[illegible]	47 [illegible]	[illegible]	[illegible]		
" Belfast,	[illegible]	[illegible]	—	[illegible]	[illegible]		
" Galway,	[illegible]	[illegible]	—	—	[illegible]		
Royal Irish Academy,	[illegible]	[illegible]	[illegible]	[illegible]	[illegible]		
Custom Buildings,	[illegible]	[illegible]	[illegible]	[illegible]	[illegible]		
Inland Revenue Buildings,	[illegible]	[illegible]	[illegible]	[illegible]	[illegible]		
Post Office Buildings,	[illegible]	[illegible]	—	[illegible]	[illegible]		
Telegraph Buildings,	[illegible]	[illegible]	—	[illegible]	[illegible]		
[illegible] Commission,	—	[illegible]	—	[illegible]	[illegible]		
[illegible] Board,	[illegible]	[illegible]	[illegible]	[illegible]	[illegible]		
Ancient Monuments (Preservation),	[illegible]	—	—	—	[illegible]		
Royal Cemetery,	[illegible]	[illegible]	—	—	[illegible]		
[illegible], Relief of Distress,	[illegible]	—	[illegible]	—	[illegible]		
Phoenix Park,	[illegible]	[illegible]	—	[illegible]	[illegible]		
St. Stephen's Green Park,	[illegible]	[illegible]	—	[illegible]	[illegible]		
Curragh of Kildare,	[illegible]	—	—	—	[illegible]		
Kingstown Harbour,	[illegible]	[illegible]	—	[illegible]	[illegible]		
Howth Harbour,	[illegible]	[illegible]	[illegible]	[illegible]	[illegible]		
Donaghadee Harbour,	[illegible]	[illegible]	—	—	[illegible]		
Dunmore Harbour,	[illegible]	[illegible]	—	—	[illegible]		
Ardglass Harbour,	[illegible]	[illegible]	—	—	[illegible]		
[illegible] Navigation,	[illegible]	—	—	—	[illegible]		
[illegible] Navigation,	[illegible]	[illegible]	[illegible]	—	[illegible]		
Phoenix Park National School,	[illegible]	—	—	—	[illegible]		

An Account showing the Receipts and Expenditure of the Commissioners

(D 1.)—PARLIAMENTARY

RECEIPTS—*continued*.	£ s. d.	£ s. d.	£ s. d.
Brought forward,	—	—	212,848 3 11
Public Buildings—continued.			
2. Railways, Ireland:—			
Vote,		69,778 0 0	
Received from National Debt Commissioners,	—	100,000 0 0	
Refunds, &c., &c.,	—	2,456 17 8	66,236 17 [illegible]
3. Tralee and Dingle Light Railway:—			
Vote,	—	—	2,000 0 0
4. Office of Public Works (Class II.):—			
Vote,	—	34,770 0 0	
Transfers or Defalcations,	—	706 13 7	
Appropriations in Aid,	—	2,024 0 2	37,500 16 9
5. Suspense Account.			
6. Relief of Distress:—			
From Lords Commissioners of H.M. Treasury, account of Civil Contingencies Fund,		—	700 0 0
7. Appropriations in Aid:—			
Public Works and Buildings:—			
Buildings:—Rents,	3,563 9 3		
Sales, &c.,	853 8 3	4,416 17 6	
Parks:—Rents for Grazing,	615 1 1		
Sales,	175 10 11	790 12 0	
Kingstown Harbour:—			
Dues,	1,298 4 4		
Rents,	387 5 10		
Water supplied to Shipping,	107 11 0		
Ballast,	34 10 0		
Hire of Planks and Cranes,	37 15 3		
" Plant,	92 0 0		
Boat Licences,	2 5 0		
Sales,	372 4 9	2,3[illegible] 10 [illegible]	
Howth Harbour:—			
Dues,	61 10 6		
Rents,	243 6 7		
Sales,	6 6 9	311 3 10	
Donaghadee Harbour:—			
Rents,	—	10 14 0	
Ardglass Harbour:—			
Rents,	6 11 0		
Dues,	144 13 8		
Sales,	4 2 10	155 7 6	
Dunmore Harbour:—			
Rents,	43 9 10		
Dues,	24 18 0	68 8 10	
Maigue Navigation:—Tolls,	—	8 2 7	
Boyne Navigation:—Tolls,	—	47 7 0	
Drainage Works—River [illegible],	—	1 18 0	8,133 10 9

of Public Works in the Year ended 31st March, 1895.

VOTES AND GRANTS—continued.

EXPENDITURE—continued.	£ s. d.	£ s. d.	£ s. d.
Brought forward,	—	693,225 3 5	2,279 3 3
1. Public Buildings—continued. Drainage Works—River Shannon,	—	3,816 10 10	[illegible],738 14 6
2. Railways, Ireland:—			
Repayments to Baronies under Tramways and Public Companies Act of 1883,	—	21,240 8 0	
Light Railways (Ireland) Act, 1889, 52 & 53 Vic., c. 66,	—	110,211 0 4	
Instalments of Annuities in repayment of Advances by the National Debt Commissioners,	—	40,043 9 0	
			171,494 16 4
3. Tralee and Dingle Light Railway:— Compassionate Grant,	—	—	2,300 0 0
4. Office of Public Works (Class II.):—			
Salaries,	25,915 6 8		
Travelling Expenses,	3,149 19 7		
Incidental Expenses,	246 11 3		
Land Improvement and Land Law Act Loans Expenses,	7,770 1 6		
		37,091 4 9	
Appropriations in Aid—Refunds,	—	104 15 3	
			37,981 2 0
5. Suspense Account:— Galway and Clifden Light Railway,	—	—	1,876 0 0
6. Relief of Distress:— To Civil Engineers, per Midland Great Western Railway, for Extra Services on Works for Relief of Distress—Light Railways,	—	—	100 0 0
7. Appropriations in Aid:—			
Public Buildings:— Taxes refunded, Costs, &c.	—	31 3 4	
Howth Harbour:— Taxes refunded, &c.	—	1 18 6	
Kingstown Harbour:—			
Cost of procuring Ballast for Shipping,	14 7 11		
Dues refunded,	6 1 10		
		20 9 9	
			68 11 7
			[illegible] 8 8

(D 2.)—An Account showing the Receipts and Expenditure of the Commissioners

PUBLIC WORKS LOANS

	£ s. d.	£ s. d.
To Balance, 1st April, 1894,	—	53,747 3 10
" Public Works Loans:—		
Vote of Credit 1893-94, £500,000—National Debt Commissioners,	50,000 0 0	
" 1894-95, £500,000—	400,000 0 0	
		450,000 0 0
		503,747 3 10

Office of Public Works, Dublin, 18th May, 1895.

of Public Works in the Year ended 31st March, 1895.

ADVANCES.

	£ s. d.	£ s. d.
By Public Works Loans,		
Amount advanced on Loans, viz.:—		
Grand Juries of Counties,	6,63[illegible] 7 1	
Public Buildings,	1,150 0 0	
Harbours, Docks, &c.,	12,856 0 0	
Railways,	3,400 0 0	
Quarries, Mines, and Miscellaneous,	300 0 0	
Housing of the Working Classes,	14,283 16 0	
Glebe Loans, 33 & 34 Vic., c. 112,	9,849 13 4	
Public Health, 37 & 38 Vic., c. 93,	132,708 6 4	
River Drainage, 26 & 27 Vic., c. 88,	8,579 8 9	
Drainage Maintenance, 29 & 30 Vic., c. 49, &c.,	21 8 7	
Post Roads, for Repairs, 6 & 7 Wm. IV., c. 116,	32[illegible] 3 1	
Land Improvement Preliminary Expenses,	1,000 0 0	
Repair of Fishery Piers,	1,019 6 8	
Seed Potatoes Supply Act, 1895,	31,932 12 8	
Lunatic Asylums Buildings, 1 & 2 Geo. IV., c. 33,	79,187 4 1	
Labourers' Acts,	80,678 0 0	
Land Improvement, 10 Vic., c. 32, &c.,	33,690 0 0	
National School Teachers' Residences,	6,135 0 0	
Dispensary Houses,	8,793 0 0	
Non-Vested Schools and Training Colleges,	3,420 0 0	
Land Law, 44 & 45 Vic., c. 49, s. 31,	26,360 0 0	
		487,716 3 7
Balance unissued,	—	16,0[illegible] 1 3
		503,747 3 10

O. W. B[illegible], Accountant.

(D 2.)—An ACCOUNT showing the RECEIPTS and EXPENDITURE of the COMMISSIONERS

PUBLIC WORKS LOANS

	Repayments (Principal and Interest.)			Totals.		
	£	s.	d.	£	s.	d.
To Public Works Loans:—						
Amounts received in repayment:—						
Grand Juries of Counties,	9,484	14	10			
Local Boards,	86,404	0	5			
Roads and Bridges,	9,750	6	8			
Inland Navigations,	6,003	0	0			
Public Buildings,	1,850	10	2			
Railways,	130,279	14	6			
Quarries, Mines, and Miscellaneous,	162	16	8			
Harbours, Docks, &c.,	18,482	18	4			
Fishery Piers and Harbours,	54	17	6			
Labourers' Dwellings in Towns,	10,891	15	1			
Artisans' Dwellings,	1,793	3	8			
Housing of the Working Classes,	22,135	11	3			
Glebe Loans,	78,181	0	9			
Public Health,	134,837	16	0			
River Drainage and Navigation, 5 & 6 Vic., c. 89,	100	0	0			
River Drainage Maintenance, 29 & 30 Vic., c. 49, &c.,	2,047	15	2			
River Drainage, 26 & 27 Vic., c. 88,	31,838	4	7			
Loans per Act 57 Geo. III., c. 34,	180	0	0			
Post Roads, Repairs,	109	6	7			
Land Improvement Preliminary Expenses,	978	3	3			
Maintenance of Navigation Works,	133	18	3			
Lunatic Asylums Buildings,	87,733	19	0			
Building Schools,	128	0	11			
Seed Supply, 1890,	10,459	7	6			
Emigration,	636	18	6			
Labourers' Acts,	67,858	18	0			
Land Improvement Loans,	99,763	4	1			
National School Teachers' Residences,	7,818	9	3			
Dispensary Houses,	6,404	16	3			
Non-Vested Schools and Training Colleges,	2,349	6	5			
Land Law, 44 & 45 Vic., c. 49, s. 31,	82,923	13	9			
Land Act Loans, 33 & 34 Vic., c. 46,	19,060	18	10			
				750,138	1	2
Church Fund Loans:—						
Land Improvements,	33,419	16	9			
Sanitary,	1,412	17	7			
Baronial Works,	18,678	9	6			
Relief of Distress,	748	9	4			
Arterial Drainage,	62	11	6			
				33,236	6	10
				783,374	6	0

Office of Public Works, Dublin, 18th May, 1895.

of Public Works, in the Year ended 31st March, 1895.

REPAYMENTS.

	£ s. d.	£ s. d.
By amount transferred to National Debt Commissioners,	—	752,136 1 2
By amount transferred to Irish Land Commissioners,	—	41,235 4 10
		793,371 6 0

G. N. [illegible], Accountant.

PRELIMINARIES, 1894-95.

EXPENDITURE.	£ s. d.	£ s. d.
Amount paid to National Debt Commissioners in Repayment of Advances,	975 3 3	
" paid for Preliminary Investigations, Advertising, Scrivenery, &c.,	1,074 3 4	2,049 6 7
Balance carried to next Account,	—	183 13 11
		2,233 0 6

G. N. [illegible], Accountant.

(D 4.)—LUNATIC

AN ACCOUNT showing the RECEIPTS and EXPENDITURE by the COMMISSIONERS of PUBLIC WORKS, IRELAND, (on 1895, pursuant to Act 1 & 2

RECEIPTS.	£ s. d.	£ s. d.	£ s. d.
Balance from last Account,	—	—	2,120 12 4
Amounts received from the Public Works Loan Fund on account of Loans to the following District Asylums, and other receipts:—			
Armagh,	2,000 0 0		
Ballinasloe,	7,069 3 0		
Belfast,	147 6 9		
(Antrim),	6,120 0 0		
Carlow,	6,000 0 0		
Castlebar,	200 0 0		
Clonmel,	3,000 0 0		
Cork,	10,000 0 0		
Killarney,	9,000 0 0		
Letterkenny,	8,000 0 0		
Limerick,	1,500 0 0		
Maryborough,	[illegible] 0 0		
Mullingar,	6,000 0 0		
Omagh,	96 14 4		
Portrane,	151 1 0		
Richmond,	3,600 0 0		
Waterford,	4,000 0 0		
Downpatrick,	510 0 0		
		79,310 6 1	
Belfast—Amount lodged by Belfast Corporation,	—	30,000 0 0	
			109,310 6 1
			111,430 18 5

Office of Public Works, Dublin, 18th May, 1895.

(D 5.)—SEA FISHERIES

AN ACCOUNT showing the RECEIPTS and EXPENDITURE by the COMMISSIONERS of PUBLIC WORKS

RECEIPTS.	£ s. d.	£ s. d.
Balance from last Account,	—	4,160 12 6
Amounts received in repayment of Loans—		
Ballydavid Pier,	43 1 4	
Liscannor Harbour,	140 15 0	
Kilkee Boat Slip,	34 9 0	
Annalong Harbour,	72 15 6	
Kilkeel Harbour,	188 19 8	
Culdaff Pier,	35 11 3	
Port Salon Pier,	101 18 8	
Portstewart Harbour,	99 6 6	
Malin Head Pier,	138 1 6	
Cleggan Pier,	219 11 10	
Carlingford Harbour,	286 13 10	
Carrigaholt Harbour,	298 11 4	
Kilmore Harbour,	214 6 9	
Ballyhalbert Pier,	128 13 6	
Clogher Head Breakwater,	603 17 8	
Seafield Pier,	109 8 0	
		2,846 12 0
		7,007 4 6

Office of Public Works, Dublin, 18th May, 1895.

ASYLUMS BUILDINGS.

Account of the Commissioners for the Control, &c., of Lunatic Asylums) during the year ended 31st March, Geo. IV., c. 33, &c., &c.

EXPENDITURE.	£ s. d.	£ s. d.	£ s. d.
Amounts expended on the following District Asylums, viz.:—			
Armagh,	8,283 18 11		
Ballinasloe,	7,080 14 6		
Belfast,	187 8 9		
" (Antrim),	5,082 8 5		
Carlow,	6,361 10 4		
Castlebar,	93 12 0		
Clonmel,	2,813 7 6		
Cork,	10,173 9 11		
Kilkenny,	8,631 14 5		
Letterkenny,	2,686 12 9		
Limerick,	1,546 6 4		
Maryborough,	2,851 14 8		
Mullingar,	2,823 16 5		
Portrane,	818 4 1		
Richmond,	5,676 3 0		
Waterford,	3,869 13 7		
Sligo,	12 17 10		
Monaghan,	258 5 6		
Downpatrick,	430 0 0		
		84,668 9 8	
Belfast,	—	19,733 18 7	
			104,401 8 3
Balance,	—	—	7,054 10 2
			111,456 18 5

G. H. Brassell, *Accountant*.

(IRELAND) COMMISSION.

Ireland, during the Year ended 31st March, 1895, pursuant to Act 46 & 47 Victoria, cap. 26.

EXPENDITURE.	£ s. d.	£ s. d.
Expenses of Engineering Staff,	479 8 5	
Amounts expended on Works:—		
Greystones Harbour,	87 0 3	
Clogher Head Breakwater,	70 13 6	
		637 2 2

(D 7.)—An Account showing the Receipts and Expenditure by the Commissioners

MISCELLANEOUS

RECEIPTS.	£ s. d.	£ s. d.	£ s. d.
To Balance from last Account,	—	—	4,[illegible] 13 0
1. Deposits for Parliamentary Expenses of Loans, &c.:— Received from Sundries,	—	—	[illegible] 9 6
2. Railway and other Arbitration Expenses, 14 & 15 Vic., c. 70:— Received from Railway Companies and others, to meet Expenses of Arbitrations,	—	—	1,[illegible] 19 [illegible]
3. Arterial Drainage Deposits, 26 & 27 Vic., c. 88, &c.:— Received from Drainage Boards on Account of Preliminary and other Expenses,	—	—	[illegible] 0 0
4. Piers—Works—1 & 2 Wm. IV.:— Lackan—Transfer from Local Loans Fund,	—	109 0 0	
Sale of Plans and Refunds,	—	3 4 11	
			112 4 11
5. Piers—Repairs—16 & 17 Vic., c. 136:— Carlingford—Transfer from Local Loans Fund,	106 11 11		
Sales of Plant, &c.,	6 4 0		
		713 18 11	
Malin Head—Transfer from Local Loans Fund,	440 14 8		
Sales of Plant, &c.,	8 13 6		
		449 7 0	
Kilkeel—Transfer from Local Loans Fund,	—	300 0 0	
[illegible]— Ditto.	—	800 0 0	
			1,[illegible] 9 11
6. Inland Navigation:— Shannon River:— Rents,	—	2,533 17 [illegible]	
Tolls,	—	2,446 1 8	
Sales, Refunds, &c.	—	6 18 3	
			4,986 11 11
7. Maintenance of Drainage Works, 29 & 30 Vic., c. 49:— [illegible] and [illegible] District,	—	—	14 3 7
Carried forward,	—	—	14,830 6 8

of Public Works, Ireland, during the Year ended 31st March, 1895.

SERVICES.

EXPENDITURE.	£ s. d.	£ s. d.	£ s. d.
1. Deposits for Preliminary Expenses of Loans, &c.:—			
Paid to Sundries,	—	—	851 10 7
2. Railway and other Arbitration Expenses, 14 & 15 Vic., c. 70:—			
Paid to Valuators, &c.,	—	—	1,189 11 11
3. Arterial Drainage Deposits, 26 & 27 Vic., c. 88, &c.:—			
Paid for Preliminary Expenses, Arbitrations, &c.,	—	—	235 10 8
4. Piers—Works—1 & 2 Wm. IV.:—			
Lackan—Labour, Materials, &c.,	—	—	90 1 8
5. Piers—Repairs—16 & 17 Vic., c. 136:—			
Carlingford—Labour, Material, &c.,	—	713 15 11	
Malin Head— Ditto,	—	145 7 0	
Kilkeel— Ditto,	—	343 13 6	
Bunowen— Ditto,	—	163 15 4	
			1,319 17 8

(D 7.)—An Account showing the Receipts and Expenditure of the Commissioners

MISCELLANEOUS

RECEIPTS—*continued.*	£ s. d.	£ s. d.	£ s. d.
Brought forward,	—	—	14,630 6 3
8. National Monuments, 32 & 33 Vic., c. 42, and 55 & 56 Vic., c. 46:—			
Dividends on Stock,	—	907 5 3	
Refunds, &c.,	—	3 0 0	
			[illegible] 5 3
9. Sea and Coast Fisheries Fund, 47 & 48 Vic., c. 21, and 54 & 55 Vic., c. 48:—	Dividends, &c.	Repayments.	
Non-congested Districts,	497 10 0	1,413 19 4	
			1,911 9 4
10. Lawes Hall, 41 Vic., c. 1:—			
Rents,	—	—	404 10 5
11. Galway Harbour Receiver's Account:—			
Dues, &c.,	—	4,123 6 7	
Sales,	—	13 9 0	
			4,136 15 7
Carried forward,	—	—	23,386 15 11

of Public Works in the Year ended 31st March, 1895.

SERVICES—continued.

EXPENDITURE—continued.	£ s. d.	£ s. d.	£ s. d.
Brought forward,	—	—	8,763 8 9
8. National Monuments, 32 & 33 Vic., c. 42, and 45 & 46 Vic., c. 46:—			
Maintenance—			
Salaries and Travelling Expenses of Architects; Caretakers' Wages, Incidents, &c.,	—	360 18 8	
Works—			
Rock of Cashel,	35 5 6		
Glendalough,	9 18 7		
Newtown Abbey,	31 18 9		
Athenry Abbey,	0 13 6		
Muckross Abbey,	87 0 1		
Yellow Towers, Trim,	4 9 8		
Sligo Abbey,	103 10 7		
Kilmallock,	80 4 0		
Kilconnell Abbey,	80 1 6		
St. Dominick's Abbey,	67 13 11		
Boyle Abbey,	342 3 8		
Mellifont Abbey,	0 18 0		
St. Columb's House, Kells,	80 17 7		
		780 8 6	
			1,141 9 11
9. Sea and Coast Fisheries Fund, 47 & 48 Vic., c. 21, and 54 & 55 Vic., c. 48:—			
Advances—Non-congested Districts,	—	—	1,883 5 1
10. Leinster Hall, 41 Vic., c. 1:—			
Rent and Salaries,	—	317 4 8	
Transfer to Her Majesty's Exchequer	—	230 0 4	
			497 4 8
11. Galway Harbour Receiver's Account:—			
Repayment of Loan,		1,871 13 0	
Salaries, Maintenance of Works, &c.,		1,871 10 4	
			3,812 8 4
Carried forward,	—	—	14,807 7 7

(D 7.)—AN ACCOUNT showing the RECEIPTS and EXPENDITURE of the COMMISSIONERS

MISCELLANEOUS

RECEIPTS—continued.	£ s. d.	£ s. d.	£ s. d.
Brought forward,	—	—	23,390 11 11
12. SOUTHERN RAILWAY:—			
Net Revenue for year ending 31st December, 1894,	—	4,070 8 6	
Amount received for payment of Baronial Guaranteed Dividends,	—	3,145 0 0	7,215 8 6
13. LETTERKENNY RAILWAY:—			
Net Revenue for year ending 31st December, 1894,	—	—	1,361 18 0
14. SUNDRY ACCOUNTS:—			
Curragh of Kildare,	—	63 16 0	
Loans Insurance,	—	848 17 6	
Land Commission (Church Property Department),	—	400 13 0	
Four Courts, Law Library,	—	5,000 0 0	
Congested Districts Board,	—	5 11 2	
Income Tax,	—	762 8 8	
Boyne Navigation Company,	—	6 10 8	
Military Cricket Club,	—	33 0 0	
Civil Service Cricket Club,	—	31 10 0	
Labourers' Dwellings Loans, Receiver's Accounts,	—	1,800 14 6	
[illegible],	—	6 5 10	
Penalties charged on overdue Instalments of Loans,	—	121 18 7	
Dublin Science and Art Committee,	—	1 0 1	
Chief Secretary's Gardens,	—	844 10 10	
Fishery Loan Fund—Interest,	—	6 10 1	
Contractors' Deposits lodged with Treasury,	—	41 0 0	
Island Bridge Waterworks,	—	15 17 5	
Drainage Works—Closing Account,	—	6 12 8	
Board of Admiralty,	—	17 10 6	
Board of Trade,	—	3 17 3	
Dividends on Stock lodged as Contractors' Security,	—	8 8 1	
Temporary Deposits,	—	7,804 8 0	17,0[illegible]

of Public Works in the year ended 31st March, 1895.

SERVICES—*continued.*

EXPENDITURE—*continued.*	£ s. d.	£ s. d.	£ s. d.
Brought forward,	—	—	16,907 7 7
12. Swilly Railway:—			
Repayment of Interest on Loan,	—	2,600 0 0	
Rent and General Charges,	—	1,437 11 4	
Dividends on Baronial (Guaranteed) Stock,	—	1,018 7 10	
			5,053 19 2
13. Letterkenny Railway:—			
Repayment of Interest on Loan,	—	1,740 0 0	
General Charges,	—	196 4 9	
			1,936 4 9
14. Suspense Accounts:—			
Curragh of Kildare,	—	63 15 0	
Linen Insurance,	—	235 3 7	
Land Commission (Church Property Department),	—	431 19 6	
Four Courts, Law Library,	—	2,407 2 11	
Congested Districts Board,	—	6 11 2	
Income Tax,	—	746 16 0	
Boyne Navigation Co.,	—	8 10 8	
City of Dublin Junction Railway,	—	46 13 10	
Military Cricket Club (from deposit by Club),	—	21 19 5	
Civil Service Cricket Club,	—	13 4 6	
Polo Ground, Phœnix Park,	—	23 18 4	
Labourers' Dwellings Loans, Receivers' Accounts,	—	1,315 8 7	
Newry Canal,	—	19 3 10	
Poundage transferred to Appropriations in aid, Office of Public Works, &c.,	—	387 12 [illegible]	
Belfast Science and Art Committee,	—	1 8 1	
Royal Dublin Society,	—	5 0 0	
Chief Secretary's Gardens,	—	463 6 0	
Fishery Loan Funds, Stamps,	—	8 2 1	
Cork and Muskerry Railway,	—	100 0 0	
Contractors' Deposits refunded,	—	43 1 3	
Island Bridge Waterworks,	—	11 4 11	
Drainage Works Closing Account,	—	9 6 7	
Board of Admiralty,	—	16 18 2	
Board of Trade,	—	65 16 4	
Dividends on Stock lodged as Contractors' Security,	—	8 3 1	
Temporary Receipts,	—	1,036 18 5	
			7,797 3 5
			60,[illegible] 16 11
Balance,	—		18,160 0 10
			48,4[illegible] 16 9

G. H. Brassell, Accountant.

(D 6.)—Arterial Drainage.—

These Works are executed by District Boards in

Schedule.—Abstract of Final Awards, and Repayments

Districts.	Counties.	Date when Award made final.	Area of Flooded or Injured Lands which have been Drained, at Ledgeward Statute Measure. A. R. P.	Cost per Acre of the Drainage, including [illegible]. £ s. d.	Increase in the Annual Letting Value of these Lands, caused by Drainage. £ s. d.	Amount of Instalment [illegible] £ s. d.	[illegible]
Athboy River,	Meath,	4th April, 18[illegible],	1,[illegible] 0 27	4 0 5	4[illegible] 18 0	—	[illegible]
[illegible],	Limerick,	2nd Oct., 1874,	178 0 5	7 1 0	93 5 1	85 6 8	11
[illegible],	Queen's,	8th Oct., 1873,	[illegible] 2 0	4 5 8	204 15 0	71 4 6	70
[illegible],	Tipperary,	9th Oct., 1871,	787 1 19	4 14 0	93 7 8	46 10 11 / 6 15 0	37 / 18
[illegible],	King's and Queen's,	8th April, 18[illegible],	2,[illegible] 1 23	2 7 5	516 14 0	—	[illegible]
[illegible] & [illegible],	Wexford,	8th Oct., 18[illegible],	3,[illegible] 2 [illegible]	3 4 10	1,[illegible] 4 7	342 10 6	[illegible]
[illegible],	Kildare,	12th Mar., 1875,	1,[illegible] 0 30	4 0 5	[illegible] 4 0	767 10 0	10
[illegible],	Limerick,	3rd April, 18[illegible],	1,017 1 [illegible]	9 13 1	6[illegible]7 17 9	3 4 4 / 106 9 9 / [illegible] 4 5	14 / [illegible] / [illegible]
[illegible],	King's,	27th Mar., 1874,	9[illegible] 3 29	5 7 1	107 12 5	68 15 9	19
[illegible] River,	Waterford,	[illegible] Sept., 1878,	[illegible] 1 [illegible]	5 5 5	[illegible]07 2 1	—	[illegible]
Bride River,	Cork,	8th Oct., 18[illegible],	1,[illegible] 0 4	6 13 8	531 5 0	184 4 6	67
[illegible],	Limerick,	26th Sept., 1878,	1,[illegible] 5 0	9 8 1	577 4 0	[illegible] 18 5	48
[illegible] River,	Tipperary,	25th May, 1872,	1,037 1 4	4 5 7	[illegible] 4 7	134 9 6	[illegible]
Cashen,	Kerry,	9th Oct., 18[illegible],	4,[illegible] 2 19	2 9 6	[illegible] 14 4	[illegible] 5 10	[illegible]
[illegible],	Kildare,	[illegible] Jan., 18[illegible],	767 3 0	6 0 5	171 12 0	—	[illegible]
[illegible],	Longford,	9th Oct., 18[illegible],	114 3 37	3 9 4	37 14 1	6 8 10	67
[illegible],	King's,	8th Oct., 1874,	[illegible] 0 30	6 5 6	140 15 4	47 6 10	[illegible]
[illegible],	Limerick,	8th Oct., 1871,	[illegible] 2 [illegible]	6 8 7	145 0 9	—	[illegible]
Douglas River,	Carlow,	31st Mar., 1875,	4,[illegible] 2 0	4 7 5	9[illegible] 16 0	[illegible] 9 6	[illegible]
[illegible],	Roscommon,	28th May, 1872,	2,[illegible] 0 13	4 11 2	1,[illegible] 1 10	[illegible] 18 4	[illegible]
[illegible],	Meath,	8th Oct., 18[illegible],	291 2 [illegible]	5 9 1	[illegible] 9 8	7 11 7 / 29 11 9	[illegible] / [illegible]
Do.,	Do.,	9th Oct., 18[illegible],	—	—	—	[illegible] 16 4	18
[illegible] River,	King's,	27th Mar., 1873,	1,[illegible] 2 0	2 5 5	414 16 0	169 7 [illegible]	19
Do.,	Do.,	4th April, 1884,	—	—	—	16 9 7	[illegible]
[illegible] and [illegible],	Meath and Dublin,	3rd April, 18[illegible],	3,[illegible] 0 11	1 0 4	4[illegible]1 9 6	4 7 6 / 100 5 9	6 / [illegible]
[illegible],	Cork,	4th April, 18[illegible],	182 1 6	10 0 4	111 16 5	21 9 9 / 61 15 10	[illegible] / [illegible]

26 & 27 Vic., c. 88, &c.

[illegible] with the Provisions of the above Acts.

[illegible], for the Year ended 31st March, 1895.

Total Amount Advanced, including [illegible] on Loan of [illegible].	Portion of Total Advanced charged to [illegible] Public Works, or [illegible] by Drainage Board.	Amount charged on Lands.	Repayments (Principal and Interest). Total to 31st March, 18[illegible].	Repayments (Principal and Interest). For year ended 31st March, 18[illegible].	Repayments (Principal and Interest). To the [illegible].	Districts.
£ s. d.	£ s. d.	£ s. d.	£ s. d.	£ s. d.	£ s. d.	
11,141 16 9	–	11,141 16 9	14,066 1[illegible] 0	—	13,9[illegible] 1[illegible] 8	[illegible] River.
1,9[illegible] 5 10	–	1,9[illegible] 5 10	1,470 10 1	44 11 6	1,4[illegible] 1 1	Ball[illegible].
[illegible] 9 9	[illegible] 10 6	2,876 16 9	1,714 6 8	142 13 10	1,[illegible] 3 1	Bally[illegible].
1,[illegible] 0 9	87 10 0 / *[illegible] 6 0	1,337 [illegible] 0	349 10 7	[illegible] 14 10	4[illegible] 16 4	Bally[illegible].
[illegible] 0 1	–	[illegible] 0 1	[illegible] 16 1	—	[illegible] 16 1	Bally[illegible].
18,[illegible] 5 6	–	18,711 5 6	3,[illegible] 2 9	[illegible] 6 1	3,[illegible] 7 6	Bally[illegible] and K[illegible].
[illegible] 1 9	[illegible] 15 2	7,[illegible] 6 6	[illegible] 17 11	[illegible] 0 6	10,[illegible] 10 5	Bal[illegible].
4,1[illegible] 17 9 / f2,[illegible] 0 0	*[illegible] 13 7 / –	7,[illegible] 5 9 / [illegible] 0 9	5,[illegible] 3 10 / [illegible] 15 1	3[illegible] 4 11 / [illegible] 11 8	3,[illegible] 19 9 / [illegible] 3 9	Ba[illegible].
2,167 3 4	–	2,167 3 4	1,[illegible] 19 1	1[illegible] 4 6	2,0[illegible] 6 1	B[illegible].
4,[illegible] 19 6	–	4,[illegible] 19 6	[illegible] 16 7	[illegible] 10 5	[illegible] 13 0	[illegible] River.
4,7[illegible] 6 8	1[illegible] 0 0	[illegible] 6 6	[illegible] 11 0	[illegible] 6 8	[illegible] 1 6	Br[illegible] River.
11,[illegible] 19 6	[illegible] 0 0	11,[illegible] 19 6	9,[illegible] 16 7	[illegible] 15 9	9,[illegible] 15 4	C[illegible].
[illegible] 11 6	–	[illegible] 11 6	[illegible] 11 7	[illegible] 11 3	[illegible] 0 10	C[illegible] River.
10,[illegible] 16 6	–	10,[illegible] 16 6	1,[illegible] 1 0	[illegible] 3 0	2,077 5 5	C[illegible].
[illegible] 13 0	–	[illegible] 13 0	[illegible] 1 8	—	[illegible] 1 6	C[illegible].
[illegible] 15 6	–	[illegible] 15 6	[illegible] 14 0	[illegible] 5 10	[illegible] 6 7	C[illegible].
2,1[illegible] [illegible] 9	46 0 0	2,[illegible] 11 9	[illegible] 17 5	[illegible] 19 0	2,4[illegible] 0 6	D[illegible].
[illegible] 0 0	–	[illegible] 0 0	[illegible] 15 6	15 14 9	[illegible] 5 11	D[illegible].
12,[illegible] 5 6	1[illegible] 0 0	12,473 6 6	14,[illegible] 0 5	[illegible] 0 0	1[illegible] 7 5	D[illegible] River.
1[illegible] 17 0	4[illegible] 0 0	1[illegible] 17 0	[illegible] 0 5	7[illegible] 1 10	[illegible] 11 2	D[illegible].
1,[illegible] 12 0	–	1,[illegible] 12 0	[illegible] 4 11	7[illegible] 0 0	4[illegible] [illegible] 11	F[illegible].
4[illegible] 12 0	46 0 0	[illegible] 15 0	1[illegible] 6 6	41 12 5	[illegible] 12 9	Do.
4,7[illegible] 6 4	[illegible] 0 0	4,[illegible] 6 4	7,[illegible] 14 1	[illegible] 16 9	4,[illegible] 16 10	F[illegible] River.
973 15 4	–	973 17 4	[illegible] 0 0	17 16 11	[illegible] 5 11	Do.
4,[illegible] 15 0	[illegible] 0 0	4,7[illegible] 15 0	[illegible] 19 6	[illegible] 4 6	4,147 0 2	G[illegible] and [illegible].
1,[illegible] 10 0	–	1,[illegible] 10 0	471 10 5	1[illegible] 0 9	[illegible] 10 7	G[illegible].
1[illegible] 15 8 / f[illegible] 0 0	[illegible] 10 5	1[illegible] 0 5	1[illegible] 0 1	[illegible] 9 3	145,077 10 [illegible]	

* [illegible] by Drainage Board, being portion of advance not expended.

f [illegible] out of the Church Fund.

(D 8.)—Arterial Drainage.—

These Works are executed by District Boards in

Schedule.—Abstract of Final Awards, and Repayments

District.	Counties.	Date when Awards made final.	Area of Flooded or Injured Lands, which have been Drained or Improved, statute Measure.	Cost per Acre of the Drainage, including Interest, &c.	Increase in the Annual Letting Value of these Lands, caused by Drainage.	Amount of Instalments payable half-yearly, to repay Cost, with Interest, &c.	[illegible]
			A. R. P.	£ s. d.	£ s. d.	£ s. d.	
	Brought forward,		65,[illegible] 0 31	—	10,[illegible] 5 6	3,[illegible] 6 11	
Greenagh,	Limerick,	4th April, 1869,	2,520 3 34	6 9 4	344 9 0	887 11 4	61
Gully,	Queen's,	4th Oct., 1874,	1,004 0 10	4 4 11	242 10 9	6— / 109 5 9	6 / 5
Gully Upper,	Queen's,	14th Mar., 1878,	409 1 18	4 13 7	190 11 1	30 8 4	40
Hogan's Pass,	Tipperary,	8th Oct., 1886,	615 1 29	9 13 0	380 14 10	181 1 3	44
Inny, Upper,	Meath, Westmeath, Longford, & Cavan,	4th April, 1891,	11,670 2 7	7 9 8	2,790 5 4	1,049 4 4	40
Island Lake and Glore River,	Mayo,	2nd April, 1873,	1,457 0 23	3 16 1	443 5 6	184 13 10	40
Kildare,	Kildare,	30th Sept., 1877,	2,347 0 30	5 11 6	400 7 10	6— / 69 1 11	6 / 17
Kilmastulla,	Tipperary,	30th July, 1879,	1,661 1 16	6 19 7	392 19 9	6—	6
Lavagh,	Meath,	2nd April, 1883,	878 1 22	7 9 7	304 13 10	137 19 0	60
Lerr River,	Kildare and Carlow,	9th Oct., 1886,	1,464 0 22	10 5 11	636 6 0	534 3 7	77
Lough Erne,	Cavan, Donegal, Fermanagh, & Monaghan,	4th April, 1891,	16,857 0 00	11 14 11	4,716 11 0	3,545 17 4	30
Do. (Navigation).	Do.,	—	—	—	—	536 4 6	34
Lough Oughter,	Cavan,	4th April, 1876,	5,077 1 00	5 1 11	840 16 8	681 3 7	34
Milford,	Cork,	4th Oct., 1867,	1,015 0 10	4 14 9	449 6 7	203 12 6	40
Morning Star, Upper,	Limerick,	4th April, 1868,	620 0 25	5 10 9	150 1 6	174 12 6	37
Mulkear River,	Limerick,	30th Sept., 1877,	5,280 9 34	9 4 1	973 0 11	367 10 7	30
Nanny River,	Meath,	4th April, 1879,	704 3 0	10 6 1	465 15 8	187 19 6	37
Do. Upper,	Do.,	4th April, 1880,	162 1 00	6 7 9	78 11 3	26 1 10	37
Owenroe,	Do.,	4th April, 1867,	2,307 2 6	5 9 9	801 7 6	178 0 11	43
Parsonstown,	Tipperary and King's,	30th Sept., 1874,	2,719 0 1	4 4 6	650 10 5	388 10 8	44
Quinagh,	Carlow,	10th Jan., 1870,	580 0 0	8 16 6	320 1 8	6—	6
Rathangan River,	Kildare,	4th April, 1883,	8,864 2 0	9 15 3	3,044 19 10	1,250 12 4	30
Rathdowney,	Queen's,	9th Oct., 1880,	410 1 38	4 0 1	189 6 4	6—	6
Silver River,	King's & Westmeath,	4th Oct., 1876,	1,888 2 09	8 17 8	215 10 6	6—	6
[illegible],	Clare,	4th April, 1871,	2,585 0 4	7 18 9	1,359 14 11	6—	6
[illegible] River,	Kildare,	9th Oct., 1884,	3,065 0 6	8 15 5	1,280 15 10	584 16 9	74
Swanlinbar,	Cavan,	23rd Mar., 1880,	345 0 19	7 6 8	166 15 9	48 5 6	36
Swilly Burn,	Donegal,	8th Oct., 1885,	1,404 2 19	6 8 1	405 5 5	118 8 10	34

26 & 27 Vic., c. 88, &c.

[illegible] with the Provisions of the above Acts.

[illegible], for the Year ended 31st March, 18[illegible].

Total Amount Advanced, including [illegible]	Portion of Total Advance charged by County [illegible]	Amount Charged on Lands	Repayments (Principal and Interest). Total to 31st March, 18[illegible]	For Year ended 31st March, 18[illegible]	To [illegible]	Names.
£ s. d.	£ s. d.	£ s. d.	£ s. d.	£ s. d.	£ s. d.	
[illegible] 10 8 / [illegible] 0 0	[illegible] 10 3	1[illegible],19[illegible] 8 5	1[illegible] 9 1	[illegible] 9 8	11[illegible] 11 4	
1[illegible] 7 0	216 0 0 / *[illegible] 13 6	1[illegible] 14 6	2,019 10 1	[illegible] 12 10	[illegible] 9 11	[illegible]
4,[illegible] 11 6	–	4,517 11 6	[illegible] 7 1	176 14 0	3,170 4 8	Gaily.
[illegible] 15 2	[illegible] 0 0	2,[illegible] 16 2	[illegible] 9	107 1 4	[illegible] 4 1	Gaily, Upper.
4,[illegible] 13 0	216 4 0 / [illegible] 0 0	4,042 8 0	[illegible] 10 9	[illegible] 4 0	2,[illegible] 0 0	[illegible] Pass.
[illegible] 3 6	2,199 13 6 / *[illegible],780 0 0	[illegible] 12 0	37,[illegible] 5 8	[illegible] 4 7	61,[illegible] 10 5	Inny, Upper.
[illegible] 13 7	116 0 0 / *120 0 0	[illegible] 13 7	7,[illegible] 15 9	[illegible] 15 0	7,[illegible] 13 0	Inland Lakes and [illegible] River.
[illegible] 4 6	200 0 0	[illegible] 4 6	10,1[illegible] 8 9	1[illegible] 0 3	10,[illegible] 9 4	[illegible]
10,[illegible] 7 8	–	10,[illegible] 7 8	1[illegible] 14 1	16 10 6	1[illegible] 0 0	[illegible]
[illegible] 13 10	35 15 4	6,191 17 6	3,010 12 9	[illegible] 9 11	1,177 9 8	[illegible]
[illegible] 8 0	[illegible] 0 0	[illegible],714 3 0	9,7[illegible] 10 0	1,1[illegible] 12 3	16,[illegible] 18 4	[illegible] River.
1[illegible] 16 0	–	1[illegible] 16 0	[illegible] 0 8	1,[illegible] 13 8	[illegible] 10 10	Lough [illegible]
17,197 14 0	17,197 14 0	Nil.	7,[illegible] 9 10	1,1[illegible] 10 10	[illegible] 2 8	Do. Navigation.
1[illegible] 4 0	–	16,1[illegible] 4 0	12,[illegible] 17 0	[illegible] 12 8	12,416 10 3	Lough [illegible]
[illegible] 14 6	–	[illegible] 14 6	2,[illegible] 10 2	[illegible] 8 3	[illegible] 6 5	[illegible]
[illegible] 0 0	[illegible] 0 0	[illegible] 0 0	[illegible] 4 5	[illegible] 17 0	[illegible] 8 6	[illegible], Upper.
[illegible] 0 0	[illegible] 1 0	[illegible] 10 0	[illegible] 17 4	[illegible] 7 0	[illegible] 6 1	[illegible] River.
[illegible] 5 7	[illegible] 0 0 / *[illegible] 13 7	[illegible] 6 0	[illegible] 16 7	[illegible] 10 10	[illegible] 15 0	Newry River.
[illegible] 10 0	–	[illegible] 10 0	[illegible] 11 11	67 11 11	[illegible] 8 10	Do. Upper.
11,[illegible] 13 6	[illegible] 16 6	11,[illegible] 16 0	4,[illegible] 10 0	[illegible] 13 7	3,[illegible] 15 4	[illegible]
11,[illegible] 17 1	1[illegible] 0 0	11,[illegible] 17 1	10,[illegible] 8 6	[illegible] 0 5	11,[illegible] 11 4	[illegible]
[illegible] 10 6	*[illegible] 0 0	[illegible] 13 8	3,[illegible] 11 1	–	[illegible] 11 1	[illegible]
[illegible] 6 8	1,1[illegible] 0 0	[illegible] 6 8	[illegible] 2 6	[illegible] 7 5	[illegible] 10 1	[illegible] River.
[illegible] 8 8	–	[illegible] 8 8	[illegible] 6 7	–	[illegible] 8 7	[illegible]
[illegible] 9 8	–	[illegible] 9 8	[illegible] 1 5	–	[illegible] 1 8	[illegible] River.
[illegible] 10 11	[illegible] 1 6	[illegible] 12 8	[illegible] 1 11	[illegible] 13 11	[illegible] 17 10	[illegible]
[illegible] 0 0	1,[illegible] 11 10 / *[illegible] 0 0	[illegible] 8 8	16,[illegible] 12 6	[illegible] 19 8	16,[illegible] 15 1	[illegible] River.
[illegible] 5 6	1[illegible] 0 0	1,[illegible] 5 8	1,[illegible] 16 6	[illegible] 5	1,[illegible] 11 11	[illegible]
[illegible] 16 6	[illegible] 18 8 / *[illegible] 0 0	[illegible] 16 0	[illegible] 9 8	[illegible] 13 6	[illegible] 8 0	[illegible] Burn.
[illegible] 8 4 / [illegible] 0 0	[illegible] 19 7	7[illegible] 8 9	[illegible] 7 3	[illegible] 11 11	[illegible] 2 7	

(D 8.)—ARTERIAL DRAINAGE.—

These Works are executed by District Boards in

ARTERIAL DRAINAGE WORKS in progress

Districts.	Counties.	Date when Award came final.	Area of Flooded or Injured Lands, which have been Drained or Improved, Statute Measure.	Cost per Acre of the Drainage, including Interest, &c.	Increase in the Annual Letting Value of these Lands, caused by Drainage.	Amount of Instalments payable each year, with Interest, after deducting Redemptions.	[illegible]
			A. R. P.	£ s. d.	£ s. d.	£ s. d.	
	Brought forward,	–	104,927 0 21	–	32,986 15 10	15,[illegible] 0 11	–
Turrent River,	Tyrone,	3rd April, 1878.	453 1 18	11 7 1	336 15 10	[illegible] 3 4	[illegible]
Tory Hill,	Limerick,	3rd April, 1878.	891 3 3	6 1 0	484 13 4	149 1 0	[illegible]
Dreenure,	Cork,	9th Sept., 1888.	380 0 17	6 8 0	243 10 6	[illegible] 14 4 [illegible] 17 10	[illegible] 11
Ward River,	Dublin and Meath,	4th April, 1888.	[illegible] 0 10	7 10 1	114 7 8	183 19 5	[illegible]
Killeen,	Cork,	8th October, 1888.	201 1 0	9 4 1	153 15 8	–	–
River Suck,	Galway and Roscommon.	–	–	–	–	–	–
Do. (Catchment Area),	Do.	–	–	–	–	–	–
	Total charge against districts,		111,[illegible] 2 0	Average 6 17 5	34,[illegible] 6 10	15,[illegible] 6 6	

Office of Public Works, Dublin, 15th May, 1895.

26 & 27 Vic., c. 88, &c.

[illegible] with the Provisions of the above Acts.

showing the Issues made to 31st March, 1894.

Total Amount [illegible] in [illegible] of Award.	Portion of Total Advances charged to Consolidated Fund for Public Works, or [illegible] by [illegible] Board.	Amount charged to Lands.	Repayments (Principal and Interest).			Localities.
			Total to 31st March, 1894.	For year ended 31st March, 1895.	To 31st March, 1895.	
£ s. d.	£ s. d.	£ s. d.	£ s. d.	£ s. d.	£ s. d.	
777,[illegible] [illegible] [illegible] / f 9,310 0 0	33,[illegible] 10 7	744,734 8 9	[illegible] 7 3	20,[illegible] 14 11	[illegible] 8 9	
3,[illegible] [illegible] [illegible]	187 10 0	3,164 11 6	5,[illegible] 18 0	[illegible] 10 [illegible]	6,[illegible] 11 [illegible]	Torrent River.
6,110 13 [illegible]	–	6,110 13 [illegible]	3,1[illegible] 8 0	1[illegible] 3 6	3,[illegible] 5 6	Tory Hill.
6,[illegible] 16 [illegible]	70 0 0	1,[illegible] 15 0	3[illegible] 9 [illegible]	184 1 0	[illegible] 10 8	Trasna.
6,[illegible] 17 [illegible]	1[illegible] 19 0	6,[illegible] 10 9	6,[illegible] 10 11	[illegible] 8 [illegible]	3,[illegible] 2 1	Ward River.
1,[illegible] 6 6	–	1,[illegible] 6 6	–	–	–	Killard.
1[illegible] [illegible] [illegible] / f 3,760 1 0	1,744 1 9	†1[illegible] 10 3	1,[illegible] 3 0	–	1,[illegible] 3 6	River Suck.
12,000 0 0	12,000 0 0	–	1,[illegible] 4 7	[illegible] 10 0	1,[illegible] 14 7	Do.
9[illegible] 2 11 / f 9,130 1 0		7[illegible] 11 4 / †1[illegible] 10 8				
[illegible] 3 11	60,177 10 [illegible]	874,716 13 7	[illegible] 10 [illegible]	31,917 10 3	[illegible] 8 9	

f Issued out of the Church Fund. † Not yet under charge.

G. H. [illegible], Accountant.

APPENDIX E.

STATEMENT showing the PURPOSES for which ADVANCES of PUBLIC MONEY are made by the COMMISSIONERS of PUBLIC WORKS in IRELAND, with the RATES of INTEREST and PERIODS of REPAYMENT.

Purpose of Loan.	Authorising Acts.	Rate of Interest per Cent.	Maximum Period of Repayment.
	LOCAL LOANS FUND.		
1. County roads, bridges, and court-houses	1 & 2 Wm. 4, c. 33, s. 23, amended by 32 & 33 Vict., c. 71, s. 1.	5	20 years.
2. Court-houses erected by the Board,	6 & 7 Wm. 4, c. 116, s. 76.	4	1 year from completion of works.
3. Bridges between counties, . .	1 & 2 Wm. 4, c. 33, amended by 4 & 5 Wm. 4, c. 61, 2 & 3 Vict., c. 50, and 30 & 31 Vict., c. 50.	5	20 years.
4. (a) Public works generally, including commercial harbours, docks, canals, and bridges other than county bridges.	1 & 2 Wm. 4, c. 33, with local or special Acts.	Not less than 4	20 years.
(b) Loans to Pier Authorities created by Shannon Act, 1885.	Shannon Act, 1885, .	3½	50 "
5. Public Buildings—			
(a) Reformatories, . . .	44 & 45 Vict., c. 79, .	3¼ 3½ 4	20 years. 30 " 35 "
(b) Public Libraries, . . .	40 & 41 Vict., c. 15 & c. 54.	5	20 "
(c) Industrial Schools, . .	48 Vict., c. 19, . .	3½	25 "
6. Railways and Tramways, . .	1 & 2 Wm. 4, c. 33, and Tramways Act, 1883.	4	35 years.
7. Fishery piers and harbours, construction of.	9 Vict. c. 3, and 29 and 30 Vict., c. 45.	5	25 years.
8. Reclamation of waste lands (see also Land Law Act, 1881).	1 & 2 Wm. 4, c. 33.	5	2 years from completion of works.
9. Housing of the working classes, .	53 & 54 Vict., c. 70, .	3¼ 3½ 3¾ *3⅞	20 years. 30 " 40 " 50 "
10. Glebe houses, erection of, and purchase of land, &c.	33 & 34 Vict., c. 112. 34 & 35 Vict., c. 100, and Expiring Laws Continuance Acts.	3½	35 years.
11. Sanitary Improvements, . .	Public Health Acts, .		
(a.) Water supply, sewerage, &c.,	37 & 38 Vict., c. 9, c. 48, and 41 & 42 Vict., c. 52.	3¼ 3½ 4	30 years. 40 " 50 "
(b.) Burial grounds, . .	41 & 42 Vict., c. 52, .	4	30 "
12. (a.) Maintenance of drainage works,	29 & 30 Vict., c. 49, .	5	Various periods, not usually exceeding 15 years.
(b.) Loans to Trustees of Districts carried out under the Act 5 & 6 Vict., c. 89.	43 & 44 Vict., c. 14, s. 18.	3½	15 years.

Purpose of Loans.	Authorising Acts.	Rate of Interest per Cent.	Maximum Period of Repayment.
13. Arterial drainage works,	26 & 27 Vict., c. 88, 28 & 29 Vict., c. 52, 37 & 38 Vict., c. 32, 43 & 44 Vict., c. 27.	4 during progress of works, subsequently 3½.	35 years.
14. Repairs of post roads and bridges,	6 & 7 Wm. 4, c. 116,	4	2 years.
15. Land improvement preliminary expenses.	10 Vict., c. 32, s. 15,	—	—
16. Repairs of fishery piers,	16 & 17 Vict., c. 136, sec. 11.	4	1 year from completion of works.
17. Maintenance of navigation works,	19 & 20 Vict., c. 62,	4	Ditto.
18. Lunatic asylums buildings, erection of, &c.	1 & 2 George 4, c. 33, 8 & 9 Vict., c. 107, 18 & 19 Vict., c. 109, 40 & 41 Vict., c. 27, and 36 & 37 Vict., c. 82.	3½	(a) 30 years.
19. Emigration,	45 & 46 Vict., c. 47,	3½ 3¼	30 years. 20 "
20. Labourers' cottages, erection of, —by boards of guardians.	46 & 47 Vict., c. 60, 48 & 49 Vict., c. 77.	3½ 3¼ 3½	[illegible]8 years. 40 " 50 "
21. Land improvement:— Loans to landlords— (a.) For sub-soiling, trenching, irrigation, embanking, fencing, and reclamation of waste lands.	10 Vict., c. 32,	(about) 3½	22 years.
(b.) For farm buildings, houses, and offices, scutch mills, labourers' dwellings, and planting.	10 Vict., c. 32, 29 & 30 Vict., c. 40,	(about) 3[illegible] 3¼	22 " 35 "
(c.) For labourers' cottages erected by order of Land Commission.	10 Vict., c. 32, s. 7, and Land Law Act, 1881, s. 19.	(about) 3¼	22 "
22. National school teachers' residences, erection of.	38 & 39 Vict., c. 82,	3½	35 years.
23. Dispensary houses, erection of,	12 & 13 Vict., c. 22,	3½	35 years.
24. Non-vested schools and training colleges, erection of.	47 & 48 Vict., c. 83,	3½	35 years.
25. Land Law Act, 1881, (a.) Loans to tenants for improvement of their holdings. (b.) Loans to Companies for reclamation of waste lands, &c.	44 & 45 Vict., c. 49, s. 31.	(about) 3[illegible] 3¼ 3½ 4 4¼	22 years. 20 " 30 " 40 " 50 "

Irish Church Fund.

For erection of fishery piers and harbours.	46 & 47 Vict., c. 26,	3¼	22 years.

Sea and Coast Fisheries Fund.

To enable fishermen to purchase and repair boats, to supply fishing gear, &c.	47 & 48 Vict., c. 21, 54 & 55 Vict., c. 48.	2½	10 years.

* Only 20 years are allowed for loans, for works not of a permanent character, for furniture, viz., fixtures, &c.

TRAMWAYS AND PUBLIC COMPANIES (IRELAND)

County.	Length of Lines.	Order in Council: Date.	Order in Council: [illegible] Capital	Order in Council: Rate of Interest	Area Charged: Designation.	Area Charged: Valuation.	[illegible]	[illegible] Capital [illegible]	[illegible]	[illegible]
2	3	4	5	6	7	8	9	10	11	12
Tyrone.	[illegible]	[illegible]	[illegible]	[illegible]	[illegible]	[illegible]	[illegible]	[illegible]	[illegible]	[illegible]
Fermanagh.					[illegible]	[illegible]	[illegible]	—	—	[illegible]
Cavan.	[illegible]	[illegible] July, [illegible]	[illegible]	[illegible]	[illegible]	[illegible]	[illegible]	[illegible]	[illegible]	[illegible]
Leitrim.					[illegible]	[illegible]	[illegible]	—	—	[illegible]
Clare.	[illegible]	[illegible] May, [illegible]	[illegible]	[illegible]	County at large.	[illegible]	[illegible]	[illegible]	[illegible]	[illegible]
					[illegible]	[illegible]				
[illegible]	[illegible]	[illegible] Feb. [illegible]	[illegible]	[illegible]	[illegible]	[illegible]	[illegible]	[illegible]		[illegible]
Cork.	[illegible]	[illegible] Feb. [illegible]	[illegible]	[illegible]	[illegible]	[illegible]	[illegible]	[illegible]	[illegible]	[illegible]
Cork.	[illegible]	[illegible] March, [illegible]	[illegible]	[illegible]	[illegible]	[illegible]	[illegible]	[illegible]	[illegible]	[illegible]
Donegal.	[illegible]	[illegible] Jan., [illegible]	[illegible]	[illegible]	[illegible]	[illegible]	[illegible]	[illegible]	[illegible]	[illegible]

F.

Act, 1883, 46 & 47 Vic., cap. 43.

Year.	First Half of Year.					Second Half of Year.					[illegible]	
	[illegible]	[illegible]	Balances, Credit.	Balances, Debit.	Treasury Contribution.	[illegible]	[illegible]	Balances, Credit.	Balances, Debit.	Treasury Contribution.	[illegible]	[illegible]
[illegible]	[illegible]	[illegible]	[illegible]	[illegible]	[illegible]	[illegible]	[illegible]	[illegible]	[illegible]	[illegible]	[illegible]	[illegible]
	[illegible]	[illegible]	[illegible]	[illegible]	[illegible]	[illegible]	[illegible]	[illegible]	[illegible]	[illegible]	[illegible]	[illegible]
[illegible]	—	[illegible]	—	—	—	[illegible]	[illegible]	[illegible]	—	[illegible]	[illegible]	[illegible]
[illegible]	[illegible]	[illegible]	—	[illegible]	[illegible]	[illegible]	[illegible]	[illegible]	—	[illegible]	[illegible]	[illegible]
[illegible]	[illegible]	[illegible]	—	[illegible]	[illegible]	[illegible]	[illegible]	[illegible]	—	[illegible]	[illegible]	[illegible]
[illegible]	[illegible]	[illegible]	—	[illegible]	[illegible]	[illegible]	[illegible]	—	[illegible]	[illegible]	[illegible]	[illegible]
[illegible]	[illegible]	[illegible]	—	[illegible]	[illegible]	[illegible]	[illegible]	[illegible]	—	[illegible]	[illegible]	[illegible]
[illegible]	[illegible]	[illegible]	—	[illegible]	[illegible]	[illegible]	[illegible]	[illegible]	—	[illegible]	[illegible]	[illegible]
[illegible]	[illegible]	[illegible]	—	[illegible]	[illegible]	[illegible]	[illegible]	[illegible]	—	[illegible]	[illegible]	[illegible]
[illegible]	[illegible]	[illegible]	—	[illegible]	[illegible]	—	—	—	—	—	—	—
[illegible]	—	—	—	—	—	—	—	—	—	[illegible]	—	—
[illegible]	[illegible]	[illegible]	—	[illegible]	[illegible]	[illegible]	[illegible]	[illegible]	—	[illegible]	[illegible]	[illegible]
[illegible]	[illegible]	[illegible]	—	[illegible]	[illegible]	[illegible]	[illegible]	—	[illegible]	[illegible]	[illegible]	[illegible]
[illegible]	[illegible]	[illegible]	—	[illegible]	[illegible]	[illegible]	[illegible]	—	[illegible]	[illegible]	[illegible]	[illegible]
[illegible]	[illegible]	[illegible]	—	[illegible]	[illegible]	[illegible]	[illegible]	—	[illegible]	[illegible]	[illegible]	[illegible]
[illegible]	[illegible]	[illegible]	—	[illegible]	[illegible]	[illegible]	[illegible]	—	[illegible]	[illegible]	[illegible]	[illegible]
[illegible]	[illegible]	[illegible]	—	[illegible]	[illegible]	[illegible]	[illegible]	[illegible]	—	[illegible]	[illegible]	[illegible]
[illegible]	[illegible]	[illegible]	[illegible]	—	[illegible]	—	—	—	—	—	—	—
[illegible]	—	—	—	—	—	[illegible]	[illegible]	[illegible]	—	[illegible]	[illegible]	[illegible]
[illegible]	[illegible]	[illegible]	—	[illegible]	[illegible]	[illegible]	[illegible]	[illegible]	—	[illegible]	[illegible]	[illegible]
[illegible]	[illegible]	[illegible]	—	[illegible]	[illegible]	[illegible]	[illegible]	[illegible]	—	[illegible]	[illegible]	[illegible]
[illegible]	[illegible]	[illegible]	—	[illegible]	[illegible]	[illegible]	[illegible]	[illegible]	—	[illegible]	[illegible]	[illegible]
[illegible]	[illegible]	[illegible]	—	[illegible]	[illegible]	[illegible]	[illegible]	[illegible]	—	[illegible]	[illegible]	[illegible]
[illegible]	[illegible]	[illegible]	—	[illegible]	[illegible]	[illegible]	[illegible]	[illegible]	—	[illegible]	[illegible]	[illegible]
[illegible]	[illegible]	[illegible]	[illegible]	—	[illegible]	[illegible]	[illegible]	[illegible]	—	[illegible]	[illegible]	[illegible]
[illegible]	[illegible]	[illegible]	[illegible]	—	[illegible]	—	—	—	—	—	—	—
	[illegible]											
[illegible]	[illegible]	[illegible]	[illegible]	—	[illegible]	[illegible]	[illegible]	[illegible]	—	[illegible]	[illegible]	[illegible]
[illegible]	[illegible]	[illegible]	[illegible]	—	[illegible]	[illegible]	[illegible]	[illegible]	—	[illegible]	[illegible]	[illegible]
[illegible]	[illegible]	[illegible]	[illegible]	—	[illegible]	[illegible]	[illegible]	[illegible]	—	[illegible]	[illegible]	[illegible]
[illegible]	[illegible]	[illegible]	[illegible]	—	[illegible]	—	—	—	—	—	—	—
[illegible]	—	—	—	—	—	[illegible]	[illegible]	—	[illegible]	[illegible]	[illegible]	[illegible]
[illegible]	[illegible]	[illegible]	—	[illegible]	[illegible]	[illegible]	[illegible]	—	[illegible]	[illegible]	[illegible]	[illegible]
[illegible]	[illegible]	[illegible]	—	[illegible]	[illegible]	[illegible]	[illegible]	—	[illegible]	[illegible]	[illegible]	[illegible]
[illegible]	[illegible]	[illegible]	—	[illegible]	[illegible]	[illegible]	[illegible]	—	[illegible]	[illegible]	[illegible]	[illegible]
[illegible]	[illegible]	[illegible]	—	[illegible]	[illegible]	[illegible]	[illegible]	—	[illegible]	[illegible]	[illegible]	[illegible]
[illegible]	[illegible]	[illegible]	—	[illegible]	[illegible]	[illegible]	[illegible]	—	[illegible]	[illegible]	[illegible]	[illegible]
[illegible]	[illegible]	[illegible]	—	[illegible]	[illegible]	[illegible]	[illegible]	—	[illegible]	[illegible]	[illegible]	[illegible]
[illegible]	[illegible]	[illegible]	—	[illegible]	[illegible]	—	—	—	—	—	—	—
[illegible]	—	—	—	—	—	[illegible]	[illegible]	[illegible]	—	[illegible]	[illegible]	[illegible]
[illegible]	[illegible]	[illegible]	[illegible]	—	[illegible]	[illegible]	[illegible]	[illegible]	—	[illegible]	[illegible]	[illegible]
[illegible]	[illegible]	[illegible]	[illegible]	—	[illegible]	[illegible]	[illegible]	[illegible]	—	[illegible]	[illegible]	[illegible]
[illegible]	[illegible]	[illegible]	[illegible]	—	[illegible]	[illegible]	[illegible]	[illegible]	—	[illegible]	[illegible]	[illegible]
[illegible]	[illegible]	[illegible]	[illegible]	—	[illegible]	[illegible]	[illegible]	[illegible]	—	[illegible]	[illegible]	[illegible]
[illegible]	[illegible]	[illegible]	[illegible]	—	[illegible]	[illegible]	[illegible]	[illegible]	—	[illegible]	[illegible]	[illegible]
[illegible]	[illegible]	[illegible]	[illegible]	—	[illegible]	—	—	—	—	—	—	—

TRAMWAYS AND PUBLIC COMPANIES (IRELAND)

	County.	Length of Lines.	Order in Council. Date.	Order in Council. Guaranteed Capital authorised.	Order in Council. Rate of Interest.	Area charged. Description.	Area charged. Valuation.	Proportion of guaranteed charged.	Guaranteed Capital paid up.	Maximum Annual Contribution.	[illegible]
[illegible]	Cork,	[illegible]	[illegible]	[illegible]	[illegible]	[illegible]	[illegible]	Full guaranteed.	[illegible]	[illegible]	[illegible]
[illegible]	Dublin,	[illegible]	[illegible]	[illegible]	5	[illegible]	[illegible]	[illegible]	[illegible]	[illegible]	[illegible]
	Wicklow,					[illegible]	[illegible]	[illegible]	—	—	[illegible]
[illegible]	Cork,	[illegible]	[illegible]	[illegible]	[illegible]	[illegible]	[illegible]	Full guaranteed.	[illegible]	[illegible]	[illegible]
[illegible]	Galway,	[illegible]	[illegible]	[illegible]	[illegible]	[illegible]	[illegible]	Full guaranteed.	[illegible]	[illegible]	[illegible]
[illegible]	Kerry,	[illegible]	[illegible]	[illegible]	4	[illegible]	[illegible]	[illegible]	[illegible]	[illegible]	[illegible]
						[illegible]	[illegible]	[illegible]			
						[illegible]	[illegible]	[illegible]			
						[illegible]	[illegible]	[illegible]			
[illegible]	Mayo,	[illegible]	[illegible]	[illegible]	[illegible]	[illegible]	[illegible]	Full guaranteed.	[illegible]	[illegible]	[illegible]
	Clare,	[illegible]	[illegible]	[illegible]	4	[illegible]	[illegible]	[illegible]	[illegible]	[illegible]	[illegible]
						[illegible]	[illegible]	[illegible]			
						[illegible]	[illegible]	[illegible]			
						[illegible]	[illegible]	[illegible]			
[illegible]	[illegible]	[illegible]	[illegible]	[illegible]	[illegible]	[illegible]	[illegible]	Full guaranteed.	—	—	—
[illegible]	Cork,	[illegible]	[illegible]	[illegible]	[illegible]	[illegible]	—	[illegible]	[illegible]	[illegible]	[illegible]
						[illegible]	—	[illegible]			
[illegible]	Donegal,	[illegible]	[illegible]	[illegible]	[illegible]	[illegible]	[illegible]	Full guaranteed.	[illegible]	[illegible]	[illegible]
[illegible]	Kerry,	[illegible]	[illegible]	[illegible]	[illegible]	[illegible]	[illegible]	Full guaranteed.	[illegible]	[illegible]	[illegible]
[illegible]	Kerry,	[illegible]	[illegible]	[illegible]	4	[illegible]	[illegible]	[illegible]	[illegible]	[illegible]	[illegible]

F.—continued.

ACT, 1883, 46 & 47 VIC., CAP. 43.

Year.	First Half of Year.					Second Half of Year.					Annual Results.				
	Receipts.	Expenditure.	Balance. Credit.	Balance. Debit.	Treasury Guarantee paid.	Receipts.	Expenditure.	Balance. Credit.	Balance. Debit.	Treasury Guarantee paid.	Receipts.	Expenditure.	Balance. Credit.	Balance. Debit.	Treasury Guarantee paid.
[illegible]	[illegible]	[illegible]	[illegible]	[illegible]	[illegible]	[illegible]	[illegible]	[illegible]	[illegible]	[illegible]	[illegible]	[illegible]	[illegible]	[illegible]	[illegible]
	£	£	£	£	£	£	£	£	£	£	£	£	£	£	£
[illegible]	[illegible]	[illegible]	[illegible]	—	[illegible]	[illegible]	[illegible]	[illegible]	—	[illegible]	[illegible]	[illegible]	[illegible]	—	[illegible]
[illegible]	[illegible]	[illegible]	[illegible]	—	[illegible]	[illegible]	[illegible]	[illegible]	—	[illegible]	[illegible]	[illegible]	[illegible]	—	[illegible]
[illegible]	[illegible]	[illegible]	[illegible]	—	[illegible]	[illegible]	[illegible]	[illegible]	—	[illegible]	[illegible]	[illegible]	[illegible]	—	[illegible]
[illegible]	[illegible]	[illegible]	[illegible]	—	[illegible]	[illegible]	[illegible]	[illegible]	—	[illegible]	[illegible]	[illegible]	[illegible]	—	[illegible]
[illegible]	[illegible]	[illegible]	[illegible]	—	[illegible]	[illegible]	[illegible]	[illegible]	—	[illegible]	[illegible]	[illegible]	[illegible]	—	[illegible]
[illegible]	[illegible]	[illegible]	[illegible]	—	[illegible]	[illegible]	[illegible]	[illegible]	—	[illegible]	[illegible]	[illegible]	[illegible]	—	[illegible]
[illegible]	[illegible]	[illegible]	[illegible]	—	[illegible]	—	—	—	—	—	—	—	—	—	—
[illegible]	—	—	—	—		[illegible]	[illegible]	[illegible]	—	[illegible]	[illegible]	[illegible]	[illegible]		[illegible]
[illegible]	[illegible]	[illegible]	—	[illegible]	[illegible]	[illegible]	[illegible]	[illegible]	—	[illegible]	[illegible]	[illegible]	[illegible]	—	[illegible]
[illegible]	[illegible]	[illegible]	[illegible]	—	[illegible]	[illegible]	[illegible]	[illegible]	—	[illegible]	[illegible]	[illegible]	[illegible]	—	[illegible]
[illegible]	[illegible]	[illegible]	[illegible]	—	[illegible]	[illegible]	[illegible]	[illegible]	—	[illegible]	[illegible]	[illegible]	[illegible]	—	[illegible]
[illegible]	[illegible]	[illegible]	[illegible]	—	[illegible]	[illegible]	[illegible]	[illegible]	—	[illegible]	[illegible]	[illegible]	[illegible]	—	[illegible]
[illegible]	[illegible]	[illegible]	[illegible]	—	[illegible]	[illegible]	[illegible]	[illegible]	—	[illegible]	[illegible]	[illegible]	[illegible]	—	[illegible]
[illegible]	—	—	—	—	—	[illegible]	[illegible]	—	[illegible]	[illegible]	[illegible]	[illegible]	—	[illegible]	[illegible]
[illegible]	[illegible]	[illegible]	—	[illegible]	[illegible]	[illegible]	[illegible]	—	[illegible]	[illegible]	[illegible]	[illegible]	—	[illegible]	[illegible]
[illegible]	[illegible]	[illegible]	—	[illegible]	[illegible]	[illegible]	[illegible]	—	[illegible]	[illegible]	[illegible]	[illegible]	—	[illegible]	[illegible]
[illegible]	[illegible]	[illegible]	—	[illegible]	[illegible]	[illegible]	[illegible]	—	[illegible]	[illegible]	[illegible]	[illegible]	—	[illegible]	[illegible]
[illegible]	[illegible]	[illegible]	—	[illegible]	[illegible]	—	—	—	—	—	—	—	—	—	—
[illegible]	[illegible]	[illegible]	[illegible]	—	[illegible]	[illegible]	[illegible]	[illegible]	—	[illegible]	[illegible]	[illegible]	[illegible]	—	[illegible]
[illegible]	[illegible]	[illegible]	[illegible]	—	[illegible]	[illegible]	[illegible]	[illegible]	—	[illegible]	[illegible]	[illegible]	[illegible]	—	[illegible]
[illegible]	[illegible]	[illegible]	[illegible]	—	[illegible]	[illegible]	[illegible]	[illegible]	—	[illegible]	[illegible]	[illegible]	[illegible]	—	[illegible]
[illegible]	[illegible]	[illegible]	[illegible]	—	[illegible]	—	—	—	—	—	—	—	—	—	—
[illegible]	[illegible]	[illegible]	—	[illegible]	[illegible]	[illegible]	[illegible]	—	[illegible]	[illegible]	[illegible]	[illegible]	—	[illegible]	[illegible]
[illegible]	[illegible]	[illegible]	—	[illegible]	[illegible]	[illegible]	[illegible]	—	[illegible]	[illegible]	[illegible]	[illegible]	—	[illegible]	[illegible]
[illegible]	[illegible]	[illegible]	—	[illegible]	[illegible]	[illegible]	[illegible]	—	[illegible]	[illegible]	[illegible]	[illegible]	—	[illegible]	[illegible]
[illegible]	[illegible]	[illegible]	[illegible]	—	[illegible]	[illegible]	[illegible]	[illegible]	—	[illegible]	[illegible]	[illegible]	[illegible]	—	[illegible]
[illegible]	[illegible]	[illegible]	[illegible]	—	[illegible]	—	—	—	—	—	—	—	—	—	—
[illegible]	[illegible]	[illegible]	—	[illegible]	[illegible]	[illegible]	[illegible]	[illegible]	—	[illegible]	[illegible]	[illegible]	—	[illegible]	[illegible]
[illegible]	[illegible]	[illegible]	—	[illegible]	[illegible]	—	—	—	—	—	—	—	—	—	—
—	—	—	—	—	—	—	—	—	—	—	—	—	—	—	—
[illegible]	[illegible]	[illegible]	[illegible]	—	[illegible]	[illegible]	[illegible]		[illegible]	[illegible]	[illegible]	[illegible]	—	[illegible]	[illegible]
[illegible]	[illegible]	[illegible]	—	[illegible]	[illegible]	—	—	—	—	—	—	—	—	—	—
[illegible]	—	—	—	—	—	[illegible]	[illegible]	—	[illegible]	[illegible]	[illegible]	[illegible]	—	[illegible]	[illegible]
[illegible]	[illegible]	[illegible]	—	[illegible]	[illegible]	—	—	—	—	—	—	—	—	—	—
[illegible]	—	—	—	—	—	[illegible]	[illegible]	—	[illegible]	[illegible]	[illegible]	[illegible]	—	[illegible]	[illegible]
[illegible]	[illegible]	[illegible]	—	[illegible]	[illegible]	—	—	—	—	—	—	—	—	—	—
[illegible]	—	—	—	—	—	[illegible]	[illegible]	—	[illegible]	[illegible]	[illegible]	[illegible]	—	[illegible]	[illegible]
[illegible]	[illegible]	[illegible]	—	[illegible]	[illegible]	—	—	—	—	—	—	—	—	—	—

APPENDIX G.

[illegible]

[illegible]

Kingstown Harbour.

Summary of Rainfall and Tidal Observations.

Months.	Rain.				Tides.					
	Fall in inches during month.	Maximum in Twenty-four Hours.		Number of days on which rain fell.	Maximum at High Water.			Maximum at Low Water.		
		Date.	Fall in inches.		Date.	Height.	Wind.	Date.	Height.	Wind.
1894.						Ft. In.			Ft. In.	
April,	3·03	16	0·63	18	7	12 8	N.E.	19	-0 8	S.E.
May,	2·00	15	1·20	18	7	12 6	N.W.	8	-0 7	S.W.
June,	1·40	18	0·41	11	6	12 8	N.	7	calm.	N.W.
July,	0·83	24	1·10	17	5	11 9	S.W.	7	calm.	S.
August,	3·45	26	1·01	25	3	12 8	N.W.	4	-0 5	N.W.
September,	0·86	28	0·25	6	20	12 0	E.	1	calm.	N.W.
October,	3·94	21	1·45	14	20	12 6	W.	3	calm.	S.
November,	1·30	1	0·25	12	17	12 7	S.W.	13	+1 3	S.W.
December,	1·39	24	0·28	13	13	12 0	S.W.	12	+1 6	S.W.
1895.										
January,	4·67	15	1·10	16	15	12 8	E.	10	+1 4	S.E.
February,	0·12	1	0·8	3	11	11 2	S.	21	+0 10	N.W.
March,	0·42	8	0·7	12	14	12 9	N.E.	11	calm.	S.
Total,	23·03		9·83	143						

The annual fishery return to April, 1895, shows there were 10,911 hampers landed in the year, as against 10,072 to same date in 1894, an increase of 839.

The number of boats remained about the same, namely 30.

Besides the fish landed here by these boats they landed large quantities at Skerries and Howth.

The fishermen consider they have had a very good season.

The local long-line fishing has been better than it has been for several years.

The herring and mackerel fishing for the local boats was very bad.

No lobsters or crabs are caught here, but prawns are got by the trawlers.

Kingstown Harbour—*Annual Return of Fish.*

Month.	Amount.	No. of Hampers.
	£ s. d.	
March,	382 11 6	371
April,	1,113 18 0	608
May,	1,949 3 0	945
June,	1,429 19 0	767
July,	1,667 10 0	897
August,	1,673 0 0	1,745
September,	2,174 16 0	1,879
October,	815 8 0	821
November,	1,971 6 6	1,361
December,	638 6 0	486
January,	652 9 0	601
February,	425 6 0	496
Total,	14,469 19 6	10,911

Howth Harbour.

The imports to Howth Harbour for the past year show a considerable increase in coal, the total quantity was 4,171 tons being an increase of 1,738 tons over the previous year.

The exports were nil.

The hook-line fishing has been very successful, and closely followed the entire year. The total quantity of line fish caught was 15,811 cleaves, which sold for £12,556 4s., being an average of 15s. 10½d. per cleave.

The herring fishing was again a complete failure. Several Scotch boats tried the fishing on their way home from the fishing in the South of Ireland, but were unsuccessful. The number of mease landed was 27, which sold for £18 14s. 6d., being an average of 13s. 10d. per mease.

The total money realized for fish sold was:—

	£	s.	d.
Hooked Fish, ...	12,556	4	0
Herrings, ...	18	14	6
	12,574	18	6

being an increase of £1,548 10s. 6d. over the previous year.

The Harbour is frequently used during the winter months by a considerable number of Dublin (Ringsend) trawlers as a port of refuge, also by trading vessels seeking shelter and waiting for tides to get into Malahide and Rogerstown.

Ardglass.

Herring Fishing.

Herring fishing commenced on 22nd May and continued up to 12th October, and there was no improvement on previous years, either in quantity or quality or price, in fact the take was less by 973 mease than the take of the previous year. The total capture for this year was 7,762 mease, and the total value £5,176 19s. 9d. The price during the season ranged from 8s. to 40s. per mease, the average price being 13s. 4d. per mease.

Number of boats fishing from the station equal 33 Scotch, 24 Manx, and 95 Irish, in all equal to 152 boats or 33 less than the previous year.

Mixed Fish.—Hand-Line and Trawling.

During the past year hand-line fishing increased here very much. At times, 11 yawls (nearly all new) were engaged at it, and about 16 of the large sized herring boats belonging to this neighbourhood were engaged at trawling. The quantity of mixed fish sold at this port during the year was about 219 tons, and the estimated amount received equal to £2,090 12s. 10d., but this would not represent the total amount earned as the trawlers frequently sold their fish at other ports. The great increase in the number of hand-line fishermen at this place is caused by the return of the haddock to this part of the coast.

Shipping to and from the Port of Ardglass during the year ending 31st March, 1895.

—	Registered Tonnage.	Cargo Tonnage.	Description of Cargo.	Observations.
8 Sailing Vessels, . 1 Steamer, .	711	1,458	Coal, . . .	Arrived and Discharged.
3 Sailing Vessels, . 9 Steamers, .	906	1,673	Potatoes, . . .	Arrived and Shipped.
1 do., . .	47	110	Salt, . . .	Arrived and Discharged.
1 do., . .	131	33	Timber, . . .	do.
34	1,809	3,274		

In addition to above 12 tug boats called either for shelter or for orders.

Fourteen sailing vessels called for shelter.

Eight small steamers called for shelter.

During the year the trade of the port was a little better than last year. The cargo tonnage on coal was 333 tons more imported, and in potatoes 398 tons more exported, and in other items of salt and timber 95 tons over the sundries of last year, making in all a total of 826 cargo tons over the trade of last year.

Donaghadee Harbour, County Down.

In addition to the damage to the s.s. "Fann" two other casualties occurred in the Harbour on the 21st of December last, one to an open diving boat 15 tons register; she was filled by the waves, turned over on her beam ends, and remained in that position at her moorings until the weather moderated, when she was righted without damage.

The other to a schooner moored abreast of Lemon's wharf, her stern moorings carried away, she swung into the dock and damaged three small pleasure boats moored there; the owner of one intends suing the owner of the schooner at the next Quarter Sessions, held at Newtownards on the 5th April, for the cost of repairs.

One vessel only arrived during the year in distress, with loss of anchors, chain, cables, and part of her sails, but the Harbour authorities succeeded in berthing her without damage.

The import of coal for the year has been 16,273 tons, last year the import was 16,169 tons, increase 104 tons; no doubt the increase would have been greater, but three of the regular traders to this port were lost this year, and have not yet been replaced, their total carrying capacity was 508 tons.

The export of bricks for the year has been 287 tons, last year the export was 402 tons, a decrease this year of 115 tons. The fishing industry has been a failure at this port during the year; the failure has been caused by the stormy and unsuitable weather throughout; the grand total captured this year is 2,317 score, last year the grand total captured was 5,123 score; five mease of fresh herrings were landed and sold at 12s. 6d. per mease, and 230 mease of salt herrings at 12s. 6d. per mease, these herrings are imported from the Scotch fishing ports.

Annual Return showing the Harbour Services for the twelve months ending the 31st of March, 1895.

Shipping.—Tonnage entering the Harbour with cargoes to discharge or load:—108 vessels; 8,697 tons.

Entering the Harbour for shelter:—24 vessels; 1,053 tons.

Number of tons of coal imported:—16,273 tons.

Other merchandise imported and exported:—Imported, granite 57 tons; maize, 74 tons; scrap iron, 95 tons. Exported, bricks, 287 tons.

Fishing vessels resorting to the Harbour for shelter, their tonnage, and number of men; 7 vessels, 106 tons, 45 men.

Quantity of salt herrings landed, sold, and price sold at:—230 mease, at 12s. 6d. per mease. Total price £143 15s.

Number of tugboats, and yachts using the harbour:—Tugboats, 78; yachts, 36.

Dunmore Harbour.

The herring fishing commenced on the 2nd May, 1894, the takes were light and the quality indifferent until the 17th October, when large shoals of prime fish made their appearance. In consequence of the stormy weather the fishing had to be abandoned. This caused a serious loss both to fishermen and buyers. The amount of herring sold was only 1,315 mease.

The beam trawlers had a very poor season. This industry is failing very much of late years.

The otter trawl boats, principally Dungarvan hookers, fishing within the headlands of Waterford Harbour during the spring and summer months, were more successful. They had some large takes of prime plaice. The shell fishers who ply their calling off this part of the coast had a very poor season. Fish was scarce and prices were low. Lobsters fell as low as 7s. and crabs 1s. 6d. per dozen, respectively.

The boats engaged in the salmon fishing on the lower waters of the Suir and Barrow, the takes were light and did not improve until the season was well advanced, when large quantities of peal set in. The weirs done better than the drift nets.

The amount of fish landed and sold was as follows, viz.:—Herrings, 1,316 mease, amount realised, £637 17s. 6d.; trawl and other fish, 4,468 cwt.; amount realised, £1,550 11s. 11d.

The number of boats that fished out of the harbour for the past year were:—trawlers, Irish 15, English 8; herring boats, Irish 53, Scotch 4; lobster, Irish 7. Total tonnage 1,254 tons, men and boys 523.

The number of trading vessels that entered the harbour within the past year was 14, men employed on board 71.

The imports and exports were as follows, viz.:—

	Imports. Tons.	Exports. Tons.
[illegible]	[illegible]	—

APPENDIX H.

National and Ancient Monuments.

Irish Church Act, 1869, 32 & 33 Vic., c. 42; Ancient Monuments Protection Act, 1882, 45 & 46 Vic., c. 73; Ancient Monuments Protection Act, 1892, 55 & 56 Vic., c. 46.

The ruins vested in the Board under the Irish Church Act of 1869 and under the Act of 1882 are, generally, in a good state of preservation.

A number of additional monuments have been vested under the provisions of the Ancient Monuments Protection Act of 1892. Amongst these are—Dunbrody Abbey, Askeaton Castle, Oughterard Round Tower and Church, Roscommon Castle, Slane Abbey, St. Dominick's Church, Cashel, Sligo Abbey. Besides these there are numerous other ruins awaiting the completion of vesting orders.

BOYLE ABBEY, CO. ROSCOMMON.

The works necessary for the preservation of this Abbey were undertaken and carried out during the past year. The ivy had completely enveloped the building, and so disturbed the stones, that the whole fabric was in danger of falling. It was difficult to deal with a ruin in this condition, and the utmost care had to be taken with the work of removing the ivy, which was satisfactorily executed. The Abbey is Cistercian. From the time of its erection it suffered from attacks by contending parties, and it was finally, in Cromwellian times, converted into a barrack. The cloisters disappeared, and the cloister garth was turned into the barrack square. Many interesting discoveries have been made indicating the original plan of the building. Amongst quantities of hewn and moulded stones, are some showing traces, in the character of their sculpture and moulding, of a much earlier structure than that now in existence.

KILLOWEN ABBEY, CO. CLARE.

This Abbey was founded in 1190 by Donald O'Brien for Nuns of the Order of St. Augustine, and dedicated to St. John the Baptist. Considerable works have been carried out. The eastern windows, which were in a dilapidated condition, have been secured from further injury. The general repairs consisted of the building up of great gaps and the concreting of the tops of the walls. It was found necessary to remove much ivy in the course of the work.

ROCK OF CASHEL, CORMAC'S CHAPEL AND CATHEDRAL.

Pointing to a considerable extent has been done in order to staunch leaks in the stone roof of Cormac's Chapel. The Cathedral is in no need of further repair for the present.

ST. DOMINICK'S ABBEY, CASHEL.

The nave, aisle, and side chapel were in a lamentable state of decay. The western front was much in need of repair. Works of preservation are in progress.

MONASTERNENAGH, CO. LIMERICK.

This is a large Cistercian Abbey of Norman character, founded in 1148. Works of repair are in progress. The eastern end fell some years ago, but it is hoped that the debris will be found to contain the missing jamb and arch stones of the three-light window, part of which is standing. If this proves to be the case, the window can be reconstituted from the old materials. The heavy ivy is being removed, and other necessary repairs are in course of execution. The size of this Abbey and the ruinous condition into which it has fallen, will render its repair expensive.

ASKEATON CASTLE.

This building at which it is proposed to commence work as soon as Monasternenagh is disposed of belonged to the Earls of Desmond. It contains a fine banqueting hall and much of the keep is standing. The seventh Earl of Desmond, in 1420, founded here an Abbey for Conventual Franciscans, which is a picturesque and extensive ruin. The Castle and Abbey, with the remains of the ancient walls of the town, form a most interesting group.

Works of repair have been carried out at Athenry Abbey and Abbey Knockmoy.

www.ingramcontent.com/pod-product-compliance
Lightning Source LLC
Chambersburg PA
CBHW031456270326
41930CB00007B/1025
* 9 7 8 3 7 4 2 8 1 0 4 6 5 *